Contents

News of the world!

You can imagine the situation, can't you? It happens all the time, all over the world. A man sees his wife and his best friend together. They're in the garden, where she's holding his hand and laughing up into his face. The friend has been staying with them for nine months—and the wife is pregnant.

Would you blame the husband for putting two and two together?

The result is, inevitably, a broken friendship, a shattered marriage, and an abandoned baby.

The situation is all too common, and the human emotions are all too real, even though the characters of *The Winter's Tale* lived long ago and far away. In *their* world (where the country called 'Bohemia', which was, in fact, part of what is now the Czeck Republic, had a sea-coast), a king could consult the oracle of the classical god Apollo and a shepherdess could refer to festivities at the Christian Whitsuntide!

Shakespeare has deliberately confused geography and violated cultures in order to *distance* his play, emphasizing that it is only 'an old tale', a story to be told by the fireside on long winter evenings. Even in Shakespeare's day, remember, there was not a lot of entertainment for the dark nights—and not much artificial lighting either! Story-telling was a great art form.

But apparently simple 'old wives' tales', like fairy stories, can be deceptive. They are diminished by these descriptions, and by the low esteem in which their tellers, the 'old wives' (of either gender), are traditionally held. Because such stories are made to seem trivial, they are able to handle subjects that can be very serious, and explore issues which are too sensitive to be spoken of in everyday conversation. A special privilege is granted by their humble status—just as court jesters and television comedians, being considered fools and clowns, have licence to voice criticisms which no serious courtier or journalist would dare to utter.

When Shakespeare wrote *The Winter's Tale* the theatrical vogue was for tragicomedy, plays in which alarming events and overwhelming passions narrowly avoid their tragic catastrophes only in the nick of time. In the plays of his final period (*Pericles, Cymbeline, The Winter's Tale,* and *The Tempest*) Shakespeare followed the fashion, but his work is distinguished from that of his contemporaries by its far greater seriousness, communicated through the force of the poetry.

Leading Characters in the Play

Their names

Shakespeare found the plot of *The Winter's Tale* in a prose romance written by Robert Greene called *Pandosto*, but he did not use the same names for his characters. Instead he turned to North's translation of Plutarch's *Lives* where he found the names *Leontes, Camillus, Antigonus, Cleomenes, Dion, Polyxemus, Archidamus, Autolycus, Hermione, Aemylia* and *Paulinus*—and even, perhaps, *Synalus,* which was changed into 'Smalus' for the supposed father of the princess in 5, 1, 156! The name *Florizel* comes from a collection of romance stories, *Amadis de Grecia,* where it is given to a prince who disguises himself as a shepherd in order to woo a shepherdess who is, unknown to herself, really a princess. Shakespeare's princess is *Perdita,* and the name (which means 'the lost one') is his own.

Leontes, the king of Sicilia, appears at first to be a happily married man with a gracious wife and a lovely son, who freely welcomes and entertains the dear friend of his boyhood days. But he is suddenly overwhelmed with groundless suspicions and jealousy. His whole nature changes, and he is driven to commit outrageous deeds whose consequences he regrets for the rest of his life.

Hermione is the loving, generous wife of Leontes. Pregnant when the play opens, she is relaxed and charming until her husband accuses her of adultery and of conspiracy to murder. She defends herself with courage and magnanimity, patiently enduring the insults heaped upon her by Leontes.

Perdita is the child born to Hermione and rejected by Leontes, who denies his paternity and casts her out to be abandoned on a deserted shore in Bohemia. She is rescued and adopted by an old Shepherd, and develops into a rare beauty. Falling in love with a royal prince—Florizel—she is forced to flee from Bohemia with him, and at last returns to her father's court in Sicilia.

Camillo, the trusted counsellor and friend of Leontes—almost his 'father-confessor'—cannot obey the king when he is ordered to murder Polixenes and escapes with him to Bohemia, where he occupies the same position of trust in the court of Polixenes. After sixteen years he is again instrumental in organizing another escape when the son of Polixenes flees from the wrath of his father.

Antigonus seems unlike the other lords who surround Leontes. His speech is blunt and forthright—that of a country man rather than a courtier. He becomes the guardian of the outcast baby, but loses his life in doing this service.

Paulina, the wife of Antigonus, shares his direct manner. More than an ordinary lady-in-waiting, she is Hermione's befriender, protector, and advocate. Uncompromising in her defence of the queen, she is equally so in her guidance of Leontes throughout his sixteen years' penance.

Polixenes, the king of Bohemia, delights to recall his childhood friendship with Leontes and is horrified when his friend's jealous suspicions force him to make a hasty departure from Sicilia. When he is seen again, at the beginning of *Act 4*, he has himself become suspicious, setting spies on the activities of his son Florizel. He also displays a dangerously vindictive attitude towards those who oppose his will.

Florizel, the prince and heir to the throne of Bohemia. He loves the 'shepherdess' Perdita, despite the difference in their social status, and is not in the least daunted when his father threatens disinheritance.

The **Shepherd** who finds the infant Perdita on the shore of Bohemia is a man of natural dignity and honour. His are the great human values of charity, generosity, and hospitality, and these are in some measure shared by his son, the **Clown**, although the latter's simple-mindedness makes him a figure of fun. The fact that he is given no personal name indicates that the role was played by the comic actor of the dramatic company.

Autolycus, Shakespeare's own creation, is an honest rogue who enjoys his knavery. He performs some of the functions of the resourceful servant to the prince in *Pandosto*, but his most important service is to bring carefree laughter and enjoyment, banished by Leontes' jealous passion, back into the play.

The Winter's Tale: commentary

Act 1

Scene 1   Before the main action of *The Winter's Tale* can start, there is much that the audience must learn, and the casual conversation between Camillo and Archidamus tells us a lot—more, indeed, than the courtiers know themselves! As they chat about their kings, Leontes and Polixenes, they bring together times past, present, and to come—the boyhood of the kings, their enduring affection for each other, and the kingdom of Sicilia's hopes for its heir, 'a gentleman of the greatest promise'.

Embedded within this elegant, well-mannered discourse, however, are words capable of more than one interpretation, and certain phrases that seem to invite ironic contradiction. Camillo is sure that the affection between Leontes and Polixenes is so deeply rooted that it 'cannot choose but branch now', and he prays 'The heavens continue their loves!'. Archidamus is confident: 'I think there is not in the world either malice or matter to alter it'. But 'to branch' is not only 'to put forth branches, to extend'—it is also 'to break away from, to diverge'; subsequent events will show, with dramatic irony, that there certainly is 'malice and matter' enough in the world, and that the 'heavens' are powerless to ensure continuity of friendship in the face of suspicion and jealousy, however groundless these may be. Even in the heartwarming commendations of the young prince Mamillius there are ominous undertones—'If the king had no son . . . '

Scene 2   With a lyrical account of his sojourn in Sicilia, Polixenes makes the break from prose to verse for this complex scene where speech tones are frequently changing. He has been visiting for some time:

> Nine changes of the watery star hath been
> The shepherd's note since we have left our throne
> Without a burden.

The poetic language here introduces a pastoral element into the play, aligning it with the classical romances of ancient Greece—

whose gods are also the gods of *The Winter's Tale*. When Leontes breaks into Polixenes' rhapsody of thanksgiving the language becomes more commonplace, but the rhythm of the shared lines is steady, insisting on the harmonious relationship between the friends. Hermione easily joins in, teasing and coaxing their guest to delay his departure in words that bring in a feminine—even domestic—note: 'thwack him hence with distaffs', 'not a jar o'th'clock'.

At first Leontes stands by to listen, but at some point he must withdraw—perhaps retiring upstage to talk to courtiers or to play with his son. No stage direction is indicated in the earliest editions of the play, so a modern editor—or the director of a performance, or any individual reader—must make his/her own decision. Should Leontes remove himself just after praising his wife, 'Well said, Hermione' (line 33); or when he hears her avowal of love for him (line 44)—which will otherwise be spoken for the benefit only of the audience/reader? He is out of earshot, most probably, when Hermione playfully challenges Polixenes' oath and threatens imprisonment; certainly he does not hear her light-hearted, loving questions to Polixenes, nor his friend's more serious replies.

Polixenes describes a childhood of blissful pastoral innocence where time seemed to stand still. Maturing sexual urges brought in temptation and opportunity for sin. Secure in her own virtue, Hermione continues to tease—but Polixenes is not laughing when he responds to her with reverence: 'O my most sacred lady'.

In the midst of their innocent playfulness, Leontes comes forward to receive—apparently with mixed feelings—the news that his friend will remain a little longer in Sicilia: 'At my request he would not'. It may be that he has overheard snatches of the tête-à-tête with Polixenes, misinterpreting the plural pronouns used by Hermione to include both wives and both their husbands:

> Th'offences we have made you do we'll answer,
> If you first sinn'd with us, and that with us
> You did continue fault . . .

Hermione draws Leontes into the conversation, prompting him to recall that moment when she agreed to marry him with the declaration, 'I am yours for ever'. The recollection delights Hermione: she rejoices now in having both 'a royal husband' and 'a friend'. But the memory appears not to give Leontes the same delight, and he seems to put a false construction on 'friend'. His own words ring hollow in his ears.

It is now the turn of Hermione, with Polixenes, to draw aside (or upstage) whilst Leontes watches them. A sudden fit of madness, like a brainstorm, overwhelms him, changing his world for ever. Even his son, joining him centre-stage, cannot divert his attention.

The verse demonstrates Leontes' mental processes, beating irregularly as his heart 'dances, But not for joy—not joy'. His words fall over their own suggestions, and 'neat' (= tidy, clean) brings to mind the name for cattle, whose horns are like those of the cuckold! His obsession with what he believes to be Hermione's infidelity leads him into a nightmare world of unreality, and the other characters are surprised by his altered appearance.

He tries to cover up for himself by drawing attention to his son and recalling his own youth, but all the time he is laying traps. When he walks aside with the boy, telling Hermione to entertain Polixenes, his language is under control—with double meanings for Leontes which are shared by the audience: 'graver' means 'more worthy, more serious'—but there are ironic implications, 'dear' is both 'expensive' and 'beloved'; and Leontes intends that the deceit of the couple will be 'found', as well as their location in the garden.

As he watches the departing couple, his heated imagination rises to fever pitch. The rhythms of his speech are distorted with hysteria, the word-play becomes frantic, and the images reveal the obscene imaginings of his mind. Calling for Camillo, he tries to share his suspicions with the bewildered courtier. Camillo has seen nothing untoward and maintains his honour and loyalty with the greatest respect until Leontes renews his attack on Hermione. Forgetting his humble position, Camillo vehemently defends his 'sovereign mistress' and boldly reproves his lord and master. But Leontes is unmovable. No words are too foul to describe his wife and her conduct, whilst the betrayal—as Leontes understands it— of Polixenes demands nothing less than death. Very cleverly Camillo becomes for a moment what Leontes has just denounced him as, 'a hovering temporizer' (line 302), and speaks the words that Leontes wants to hear:

> I must believe you, sir:
> I do; and will fetch off Bohemia for't.

—although he makes conditions:

> Provided, that when he's removed, your highness
> Will take again your queen as yours at first.

He is equivocating now, using language with one meaning for Leontes and quite another meaning for himself (and the audience): 'fetch off', for instance, can mean 'do away with, kill'—and also 'take away, rescue'. 'Account me not your servant' is rich in its implications: as Leontes' *obedient* servant, Camillo will poison the cup he gives to Polixenes; as a *good* servant to Leontes, he will protect the king from his own folly by preserving Polixenes' life; or perhaps he is intending to leave Leontes' service altogether.

Camillo perfectly articulates his dilemma so that the audience/reader can be quite confident in him and his judgements. There is never any doubt in his mind—or in ours—about the innocence of Hermione and her relationship with Polixenes. Whatever madness has taken possession of Leontes' senses, it is his and his alone!

Polixenes is aware that something is wrong, and grasps the full horror of the situation when Camillo has explained it to him:

> This jealousy
> Is for a precious creature; as she's rare,
> Must it be great; and as his person's mighty,
> Must it be violent . . .

Camillo is practical. He has made all arrangements and Polixenes, willingly and trustingly, allows himself to be directed.

The action of Scene 2 is completed in less than a day: only a few hours, it would seem, have elapsed between the joyous morning of innocent friendship and the time of dark and jealous passion. In this Shakespeare varies greatly from his source, Robert Greene's novel *Pandosto*, where weeks and even months are allowed for the king's developing suspicions. Greene tells how Pandosto's wife

> Bellaria, who in her time was the flower of courtesy, willing to show how unfeignedly she loved her husband by his friend's entertainment, used him likewise so familiarly that her countenance betrayed how her mind was affected towards him, oftentimes coming herself into his bedchamber to see that nothing should be amiss to mislike him. This honest familiarity increased daily more . . . [until] . . . there grew such a secret uniting of their affections, that the one could not well be without the company of the other: in so much, that when Pandosto was busied with such urgent affairs that he could not be present with his friend Egistus, Bellaria would walk with

him to the garden, where they two in private and pleasant devices would pass away the time to both their contents . . . [Eventually] a certain melancholy passion entering the mind of Pandosto drove him into sundry and doubtful thoughts . . . He considered with himself that Egistus was a man and must needs love, that his wife was a woman, and therefore, subject unto love . . .

Act 2

Scene 1 The sudden alarms and hasty actions now give way to a scene of happy domesticity where a heavily pregnant mother plays with her little son and listens, laughing, to his tale of sprites and goblins. But their tranquillity is shattered when Leontes erupts among them, reacting with quick questioning and ejaculations of horror to the news of Polixenes' flight with Camillo. He has been betrayed—he is sure of it—by his closest friend and by his trusted servant! Once again, the movement of the verse reveals the agitation of his thoughts—the stops and starts, the abrupt changes of direction. And the violence of his nauseated imagery shows the depth of his emotion, which explodes with ever-increasing passion when his attention focuses on Hermione and her pregnancy. What her ladies, welcoming the healthy fruition of nature, have just praised as her 'goodly bulk', now becomes the object and proof of Leontes' suspicions: ' 'tis Polixenes Has made thee swell thus'.

The lady-in-waiting's word 'goodly'—perhaps half-heard by Leontes as he came into the room—is echoed by the king, insane with rage, in speeches of denunciation so well articulated by the dramatist that the actor/reader needs no further direction. Through a tortuous syntax of hints and hesitations Leontes arrives at the brutal denunciation: 'She's an adult'ress'. Hermione's horrified disclaimer only gives him pause for breath, so that he can continue his assault on her with renewed and fearful energy. Her ladies weep for her, but Hermione is dignified, accepting her predicament with saint-like resignation as some kind of trial of her spiritual strength: 'This action I now go on Is for my better grace'.

She has a stalwart champion, however, in Antigonus, who challenges Leontes in the blunt language of the farmyard. Antigonus is supported by other attendant lords, but even their combined testimony and persuasion cannot open Leontes' eyes. His jealous tyranny ('what need we Commune with you of this') still looks for their approval, however, and it is his own decision to lay the matter before the oracle. In this he wins some little, momentary praise—unlike Pandosto, who responds only to the defensive urging of his queen.

Leontes is pompous and self-righteous, but a wry comment from Antigonus is deflationary and—for the audience—reassuring. This sorry business may yet turn 'To laughter . . . If the good truth were known'.

Scene 2   The easier mood continues into the next scene when the wife of Antigonus approaches the prison where Hermione is being held. Paulina shares her husband's staunch faith in Hermione's innocence. Like Antigonus she is fearlessly outspoken, refusing to be intimidated by the authority of either Leontes or the gaoler—and the latter is willingly persuaded by the logic of her argument to release Hermione's newly-born child:

> This child was prisoner to the womb, and is
> By law and process of great nature, thence
> Freed and enfranchis'd.

Scene 3   Alone on the stage, Leontes persists in tormenting himself, interpreting the sickness of his son as the child's response to the disgrace—as he himself sees it—of Hermione. Paulina thrusts her way through to him, heard and seen by the audience well before her intrusion attracts Leontes' notice. She presents herself as the physician who would bring nature's remedy for his disordered senses—although, of course, Leontes, involved in his tortured imaginings and vengeful fantasies, will not hear her. Although he is fearful in his anger, he is also somewhat ludicrous in his petulant complaint to Antigonus,

> I charg'd thee that she [Paulina] should not come about me.
> I knew she would.

For a few lines there is squabbling, with almost comic insults, and the entire court seems to join in attempts to dissuade Leontes from his murderous purposes. But to no avail. Hermione's baby is condemned to be cast out to 'some remote and desert place', and Antigonus must execute the sentence.

Hardly has he left the stage when news is brought of the returning ambassadors from Delphos who bring the verdict of the oracle. Their speed has been remarkable, and Leontes congratulates himself on having—apparently—secured the favour of the god.

Act 3

Scene 1 The ambassadors seem to have brought with them some of the sanctity and serenity of Apollo's shrine. The solemn language and the formal rhythms of their speech are tranquillizing for the audience, leading them to hope that perhaps, for Hermione, the 'issue' will indeed be 'gracious'.

Scene 2 The action borrowed from *Pandosto* has been speeded-up in Shakespeare's play: the fiction's two trial scenes, separated by several weeks, have been fused into one.

At first Leontes shows himself most anxious to demonstrate that he is no tyrant and that the case against Hermione is being legally presented—but he is quick to interrupt and contradict her defence. His interpolations threaten to reduce the solemnity of the occasion to the level of a slanging-match, but they are sharply answered by Hermione, who is always dignified and controlled in her self-justification. She describes her feelings, but does not give way to them until the very end of the hearing. Perhaps even now the words are spoken 'aside' from the public assembly, in a soliloquy apprehended only by the audience/reader:

The Emperor of Russia was my father.
O that he were alive . . .

Into this highly-charged emotional situation the few words of the oracle drop with icy precision:

Hermione is chaste; Polixenes blameless; Camillo a true subject; Leontes a jealous tyrant . . .

There is general rejoicing—almost!

Leontes refuses to accept the judgement of the oracle, and his refusal constitutes a shocking blasphemy against the great god Apollo. Retribution is immediate. The sudden news of his son's death brings Leontes to his senses—but it is already too late. Hermione falls down, and although he gabbles out confessions of guilt and promises of amendment, Leontes must yet hear the words of Paulina.

Paulina is given a long speech in which to build up fresh suspense. Shakespeare has most skilfully orchestrated the two scenes from *Pandosto*, starting from the long, slow formality of Hermione's defence-speech to the three quick, sharp shocks of the oracle's judgement, the Servant's announcement, and Hermione's collapse. Before another climax can be achieved, there must be some respite so that Leontes, his court—and the audience—can digest the enormity of the situation. Paulina bursts into Leontes' self-reproach with loud lamentations and angry accusations which rise to a crescendo with her announcement that

> The queen, the queen,
> The sweet'st, dear'st creature's dead.

The scene subsides in general woe. Leontes is a shattered man.

Scene 3   Far away, the ship carrying Antigonus and the baby Perdita has landed on the coast of Bohemia—the kingdom of Polixenes. Much ink has been wasted, along with many jokes, to explain Bohemia's sea-coast, but the truth is—surely—very simple: the country of this play, its name suggested by the author of *Pandosto*, exists only through Shakespeare's imagination!

The tyrant king of Shakespeare's source gave no specific instructions about the disposal of his queen's infant, which was cast alone into a stormy sea and,

> being tossed with wind and wave, floated two whole days without succour, ready at every puff to be drowned in the sea, till at last the tempest ceased and the little boat was driven with the tide into the coast . . .

Shakespeare leaves less to chance—but he still leaves the audience doubtful whether the experience which guides the baby's guardian is really a ghostly visitation—as Antigonus interprets it—or only a dream.

The narration is melodramatic, but it is succeeded by comedy. In panic Antigonus rushes from the stage, pursued by a bear—an actor dressed in a bearskin. There is no need to postulate the availability of a tame bear, borrowed from the nearby bear-baiting ring or from some travelling showman! A complete change of mood is required, and verisimilitude is not important to Shakespeare at this point—otherwise this master-craftsman would have devised some less startling cue for an exit. Antigonus has served his dramatic purpose and it is essential that there should be no link, other than those things laid beside the baby (line 47), with Sicilia and the events at Leontes' court.

Horror and pity are dissolved in laughter by the Clown's recital of the scene he has just witnessed—the sudden storm, the shipwreck with the drowning of all hands on board, and the hungry bear that tore out the nobleman's shoulder-bone. Details and images are striking, but the abrupt subject-switches deflect all emotion. The amazed Shepherd listens to his son, then counters the excitement with his own discovery—and, unwittingly, utters words that open up the play's new direction: 'thou met'st with things dying, I with things new-born'.

This little scene acts as a hinge to join the two parts of the play—the tragic first movement of loss, despair, and death which started with Polixenes' half-serious lament for the outgrown innocence of childhood; and its resolution, beginning auspiciously with new birth, the discovery of good fortune—and another half-serious comment, this time from the Clown to his father: 'If the sins of your youth are forgiven you . . . '

Act 4

Scene 1   A male figure, wings on his back and an hour-glass in his hand, introduces himself as the personification of Time and proceeds to deliver a single speech in rhyming couplets. Shakespeare has set this passage apart from the main body of his play, using its old-fashioned idiom to serve more than one purpose. The speech, uttering a few commonplaces about the nature of time, allows for the crossing of the 'wide gap' of sixteen years, and functions as a bridge between the two parts of the play. Reminding the audience that he has already mentioned 'a son o'th'king's' (line 22), 'Time' seems to speak with the author's own voice—and it has even been suggested that Shakespeare himself might have acted the role when *The Winter's Tale* was first performed, personally teasing those of his listeners who were familiar with modern literary theory!

Academic critics writing at the time of Shakespeare were most insistent on the 'Three Unities'—unity of action, of place, and of time. The notion stems from Aristotle, who recommended that a play's action should be complete—with beginning, middle, and end; that the events should be performed in a single place; and that everything should happen within twenty-four hours. Aristotle's recommendations became rules for Renaissance theorists, but in *The Winter's Tale* Shakespeare seems to delight in their violation. As 'Time', he points out that there is no permanent validity in any such laws and customs: they were created in time, and they will be destroyed in time.

In his *Sonnets*, Shakespeare was much concerned with the action of Time—Time the Destroyer:

> When I have seen by time's fell hand defaced
> The rich, proud cost of outworn buried age . . .
>
> (Sonnet 64)

> When forty winters shall besiege thy brow,
> And dig deep trenches in thy beauty's field . . .
>
> (Sonnet 2)

Now he takes as his starting-point a novel whose subtitle is '*The Triumph of Time*',

> Wherein is discovered by a pleasant history that although by the means of sinister fortune truth may be concealed, yet by Time, in spite of fortune, it is most manifestly revealed . . .

The novel celebrates Time as the father of Truth, and the Chorus promises that the play will do the same. *The Winter's Tale*, however, has more to offer than *Pandosto*: 'but let Time's news Be known when 'tis brought forth'.

Scene 2   The second part of the play, like a mirror-image of the first, opens with a scene in the formal language of courtly prose. After an exile of sixteen years in a foreign land, Camillo (probably not a young man when he left Sicilia) is homesick for his own country. He has become to Polixenes what he was to Leontes—guide, counsellor, and friend, his 'right-hand man'. But Polixenes is selfish in his dependency, and he has the power to silence Camillo's longings with his own anxieties. The polite exchange masks a stern reality: the suspicious king has set secret agents to watch his own son, and he will not scruple to disguise himself and, with Camillo as his accomplice, carry on spying!

Scene 3   The tensions of the court are quickly dispersed by the carefree song of an honest rascal. Autolycus is Shakespeare's own creation: as a character he has no counterpart in the source of the play, although he has some of the wiliness and performs some of the functions of Capnio, the prince's manservant. Wittily explaining himself and his 'profession' (fired from the prince's service, he lives by petty pilfering), Autolycus prepares the audience for some more welcome laughter. The warm-hearted Clown is easily conned out of his money—and Autolycus gets more than his purse from him. The sheep-shearing feast is now the focus of his—and the audience's—attention.

Scene 4   The country folk have assembled for their annual feast. Among them, but outstanding in every way, are Perdita and the prince Florizel. Perdita is dressed as queen of the feast, garlanded like the goddess Flora, and Florizel (who has disguised himself as 'Doricles', a 'shepherd swain') approves her costume—although Perdita herself is embarrassed by it. She abhors pretence of any sort, accepting her role as mistress of the feast because it is her father's will and allowing herself to be 'most goddess-like pranked up' only to satisfy tradition. Florizel's poetic hyperbole, invoking the examples of amorous gods, gets only practical commonsense in response. But her father chides her shy retirement, comparing it with his wife's former bustling energy.

Two strangers have appeared at the festivities. The audience, of course, recognizes Polixenes and Camillo, but the stage conventions of Shakespeare's theatre insisted that any disguise must be impenetrable for other characters—and so Florizel does not know his own father!

Obedient to her father's urging of country hospitality, Perdita steps forward gracefully with flowers to welcome the strangers as guests and friends. She indicates 'rosemary and rue', herbs that will keep fresh 'all winter long'.

Accepting them, Polixenes (who, being the same age as Leontes, must now be about 46) suggests that these 'flowers of winter' have been selected as appropriate for old men—'well you fit our ages'—but Perdita is quick to repudiate the suggestion. It's a difficult time of year for flowers, she explains: carnations and pinks ('streaked gillyvors') are the only ones in season, but she doesn't grow hybrids like these in *her* garden. Polixenes is interested, and Perdita gives her reason: she will not try to improve on nature!

The disguised king wants to debate the issue, arguing that man and his powers are themselves natural creations. The idea was a commonplace of the Renaissance, but the king's horticultural instance is fraught with irony for the present situation. Perdita refuses to be drawn into an argument, politely conceding the point to Polixenes—but rejecting any application to herself and her garden.

Now, however, she has found the proper floral tributes for 'men of middle age'—although she must lament the lack of spring flowers which would compliment the youth of Florizel and the shepherdesses. Perdita establishes herself in this passage as a strong character and a very powerful force in the overall scheme of the play. To present innocence, charm, and modesty on the stage is no easy task for a dramatist (or an actress), but here Shakespeare writes lines of such lyrical beauty, varied with quick laughter, that there is no risk of losing the lively individual personality in the aggregation of her virtues. The sensible, practical Camillo is fascinated and moved to poetic wonderment—

> I should leave grazing, were I of your flock,
> And only live by gazing—

but Perdita discounts his flattery:

> Out, alas!
> You'd be so lean that blasts of January
> Would blow you through and through.

Perdita invokes Proserpina, daughter of Ceres, goddess of harvests. Proserpina was snatched away from her Sicilian home by Pluto (Dis in Greek mythology), god of the underworld. Her distraught mother went up and down the world in search of her, and winter spread over the face of the earth. Only when a bargain was reached with Pluto—that Proserpina should be restored for six months of each year—did spring return to the earth. Once the association of Perdita and Proserpina (with all its implications for spring, new birth, and re-creation) has been established, Shakespeare does not labour his point.

More classical allusions enrich Perdita's verse as it generates images of delicate spring flowers in lines of consummate artistry. Sight co-operates with sound in the repeated sibilants and labials of 'swallow', 'sweeter', 'strength'; 'violets', 'lids', 'pale', 'behold'; and the rhythm seems to enact the very movement of spring, at first tentative and then boldly confident, like the

> Daffodils,
> That come before the swallow dares, and take
> The winds of March with beauty.

The lyric moment, like the season, is fleeting: the goddess becomes a girl again, hugging her lover 'quick, and in [her] arms', and laughing at her play-acting. Classical mythology is abandoned for the familiar (to Shakespeare's audience) 'Whitsun pastorals' and the bustle of English rural festivities—although not before Florizel has remarked the unique perfection of everything that Perdita does and is, with a perception that is (perhaps reluctantly) shared by Polixenes:

> nothing she does or seems
> But smacks of something greater than herself,
> Too noble for this place.

But it is time for amusement—and some serious talking. The 'pedlar at the door' proves to be Autolycus, come to make still more profit from his earlier encounter with the Clown. The country folk welcome him with excitement, rifling his pack for its trumpery knick-knacks and revelling in his ballads—parodies of those sold in Shakespeare's contemporary England.

The gaiety reaches its height with the arrival of dancers, some of them professional ones (and perhaps even recognizable as members of Shakespeare's company) who have 'danced before the king'.

Whilst the revellers—and the audience—are being entertained by the dancing 'satyrs', Polixenes has drawn the Shepherd aside for some 'sad talk'. Now he comes forward with some apparently light-hearted questioning for 'Doricles'. The young lover speaks fervently of his love for Perdita and his determination to make her his wife. Despite the warnings of Polixenes, he refuses to seek his father's permission. The audience—knowing the full situation—wait in suspense for the revelation that must come.

Polixenes explodes in fury. He threatens disinheritance to his son; death to the Shepherd; and defilement to Perdita. The fit is momentary—and the sentence is deferred. But the fun is ended: the party is over.

After Polixenes has stormed out, Perdita speaks into the silence. She 'was not much afeard', yet she is resigned to the sacrifice of her love. But Florizel is undaunted and, recognizing Camillo for the first time, takes the courtier into his confidence and declares his intention to escape from his father's wrath. 'Where are you going?' 'I don't know—anywhere!' Camillo seizes on this uncertainty and quickly turns it to his own purpose, curbing the headstrong Florizel with tact and diplomacy, and manipulating the actions of the other characters as though he were himself the author of their play: 'as if The scene you play were mine'.

Another break for laughter. Autolycus is at hand to divert the audience whilst Camillo organizes the lovers into his plot—which finds use also for the rogue pedlar. More disguise is needed, despite Perdita's reluctance to appear other than she really is—or that she *thinks* she is!

In his pedlar's attire, Autolycus was unrecognized by either the Clown (the victim of his con-trick) or Florizel (his former master). Now in another change of dress, he is able to pass himself off as a courtier to the bewildered Shepherd and his son. Showing an unexpected streak of loyalty to the prince, Autolycus sets out to delay their passage to the king—and, of course, to get what he can for himself out of the situation.

The elements of this complex and complicated scene are mainly present in *Pandosto*—the country feast, the young lovers, the escape from parental wrath with the aid of a crafty servant—but Shakespeare has crafted them into a very different whole.

Act 5

Scene 1   From our privileged position in the audience, we have observed the workings of Time (under, it would seem, the direction of some careful Providence) and now, as the scene returns to Sicilia, we can look forward with confidence to a fortunate issue out of his troubles for Leontes, and a happy ending for the play. First, though, we need to see how Leontes has (unknowingly) prepared himself to receive this blessing.

Cleomenes has no doubt that the period—sixteen years—of mourning has been fully accomplished and that Leontes has attained a state of grace that is 'saint-like'. The courtier's words echo those of *The Book of Common Prayer*, 'O most merciful God, which . . . dost so put away the sins of those which truly repent, that thou rememberest them no more . . . ' ('For the Visitation of the Sick'). But Leontes cannot forget: his confession of guilt and responsibility is made in the simplest language and with rhythms that, unobtrusively, stress the full meanings of the words—'The wrong I did myself: which was so much', 'heirless', 'Destroyed', 'Bred'.

Dion, with the welfare of the kingdom at heart, urges the king to consider remarriage, but Paulina, who has been ever-present with him in his grief and is still uncompromising in her speech, reminds Leontes of Hermione, 'she you killed'. Paulina is attentive to the message of the oracle, which was—as the audience knows— more than simple prophecy:

> . . . the king shall live without an heir, if that which is lost be not found.

Her reminiscences stimulate those of Leontes, and together they seem to conjure up the very spirit of Hermione to become a living presence.

A moment's stillness follows Leontes' promise to Paulina— 'We shall not marry till thou bids't us'—and then the audience's expectations (and the king's obedience) are given their reward. The arrival of Florizel and Perdita is 'as welcome As is the spring to th'earth', bringing life to the dead land and hope for the future— although nothing can erase the past from Leontes' thoughts:

> What might I have been,
> Might I a son and daughter now have look'd on,
> Such goodly things as you!

The words speak a grief that the audience must feel, even though the poignancy is lessened by the ironic detachment of our foreknowledge—which also reduces the threat when we hear of the arrival of Polixenes in hot pursuit of the runaway lovers.

On learning that the two young people are in fact not married, Leontes promises to plead for Florizel and—attempting a joke—for

Perdita, who has quite captivated him. Paulina is quick to put a stop to any nonsense: 'Your eye hath too much youth in't'. She reminds him of Hermione, who 'was more worth such gazes Than what you look on now'. Leontes had not forgotten: 'I thought of her, Even in these looks I made'. The incident was suggested by *Pandosto*, where the king, 'contrary to his aged years, began to be somewhat tickled with the beauty of Fawnia'. Shakespeare takes the matter no further (unlike his source), and he hurries his characters off the stage, depriving the audience of the grand recognition scene that (we feel) we have been entitled to expect.

Scene 2   Instead, we have a narration of events which is handled with masterly skill. Autolycus 'stands in' for the audience to hear the reports of three courtiers, each with something new to add. The first tells of the meeting of the kings, in words suggestive of something more than an ordinary reunion and reconciliation: 'They looked as they had heard of a world ransomed, or one destroyed'. Rogero, the second courtier, announces the discovery of Perdita's identity: it was just like an old story come true, and a real subject for the popular press (i.e. the ballad-makers whose wares had stuffed the pedlar's pack at the sheep-shearing feast). The unlikelihood of the story is emphasized by the third Gentleman, who has seen all the circumstantial evidence for its truth, and has heard the incredible details of the death of Antigonus—which was also 'Like an old tale'! The play's characters become ever more convincing and 'real' the more they invoke fictions at a still further remove, and existing on yet another plane of reality.

The scene, like the matter it relates, swings between laughter and tears—between the comic, the sentimental and the melodramatic. The actual events would have been too much for any onstage presentation!

Unmitigated laughter brings the scene to an end, gently satirizing social pretensions as well as the Clown's simplicity. For the Shepherd, the change of status demands a change of conduct: 'we must *be* gentle, now we are gentlemen'. His son, however, delights in outward trappings ('See you these clothes?') and greater licence ('If it be ne'er so false, a true gentleman may swear it'). In Shakespeare's day, class distinctions, once fixed and definite, were being eroded: in the first audiences of *The Winter's Tale* there would doubtless be many 'gentlemen' who had not been 'gentlemen born', a rank formerly allowed only to those who could claim descent (on both sides) from three generations of gentry.

Scene 3 Formal courtesy returns as Leontes and Paulina exchange conventional, but sincerely meant, politenesses. Leontes has been given a tour of the art gallery, and he is properly appreciative—but this is not what he came to see. At last Paulina shows the pride of her collection, a statue of Hermione which stands 'Lonely, apart'. The audience has not been expecting this episode and (like the characters on stage) must be directed by Paulina at first to silent wonder ('I like your silence, it the more shows off Your wonder'), and then to a closer examination ('But yet, Paulina, Hermione was not so much wrinkled').

Leontes stands as still as the stone he is looking at, but Perdita wants to touch. Paulina gently holds her back, and at the same time leads Leontes' thoughts forward: 'your fancy May think anon it moves', 'He'll think anon it lives'. It seems that magic is in the air, but Paulina repudiates any suggestion of 'unlawful business'.

Music creates one spell and breaks another, holding the onlookers in a charmed stillness and releasing Hermione from the silence of sixteen years. Her movements are slow and apparently hesitant ('nay, come away . . . she stirs'), and Leontes evidently draws back, needing Paulina's encouragement ('Start not . . . Do not shun her . . . present your hand'). After his first gasp of amazement ('O, she's warm!'), Leontes' actions, described by those who stand by, speak louder than words—and Hermione still says nothing until Paulina, herself like a proud mother, presents 'Our Perdita' to her.

This scene never fails! I have heard—and *felt*—the breathless, expectant silence of the most sophisticated audiences at Stratford-upon-Avon, wondering at the mystery. Many in these audiences have been scholars, critics, and lecturers who know all about the play and who have read it and seen it, edited, criticized, and taught it—but all knowledge is forgotten, and all disbelief willingly suspended, before the legitimate magic of Shakespeare's theatre.

Once mother and daughter have been united there is no time—and no need—for any further explanation. The highly charged emotional atmosphere is relaxed by Paulina who dismisses these 'precious winners all' to an 'exultation' which she herself cannot 'partake'. The note of sadness is short-lived. By supplying a match—Camillo—for Paulina, Leontes satisfies comedy's demands for harmonious completeness, and the play is ended.

Fantastic!

'This news, which is called true, is so like an old tale that the verity of it is in strong suspicion.' As the amazing events unfold before them in *Act 5*, the Gentlemen at Leontes' court are taken completely by surprise—but not so the audience. We have been expecting this—anticipating the end of the play from (almost) the very beginning! Shakespeare has kept us 'in the know' all the time, showing us how everything works. This is really what distinguishes Shakespeare's last plays (*Pericles*, *Cymbeline*, *The Winter's Tale*, and *The Tempest*) from the tragicomedies written by his contemporaries. The happy ending in their plays often seems to have been imposed at the last minute by the dramatist's artificial means, but here in *The Winter's Tale* events which have been properly understood by the audience/readers develop in such a way as to achieve the desired conclusion quite naturally.

Look at the way Shakespeare has planted signs, like clues in a detective story, all along the way—although some of them might have been missed, or misinterpreted. First there was the anonymous Gentleman who described the love between Leontes and Polixenes, an affection so profound that it 'cannot choose but *branch* now' (*1*, 1, 24). *Branch*—meaning 'stretch out, bear fruit', or 'diverge, split up'? Then there was the subtle disclosure that Polixenes had been visiting in Sicilia through 'Nine changes of the watery star'—time enough to account for Hermione's pregnancy . . .

Gradually we learned to trust and be guided by two characters, Antigonus and Camillo. As the jealous storm-clouds gathered over Leontes' court, the audience was comforted by the assurance from Antigonus that the whole sorry business might well turn 'To laughter . . . If the good truth were known' (*2*, 1, 198–9). Ironically, it was the death of Antigonus that swung the audience's mood: the direction that saw him off the stage, *Exit, pursued by a bear*, was the cue for the laughter to start!

The Chorus-like figure of Time, bridging the wide gap of sixteen years, admitted the audience even more fully into Shakespeare's confidence. Camillo was a welcoming presence in Bohemia, and his declared longing to return to his native land was a pointer to the route that the action would take—despite Polixenes' resistance. Like a guardian angel, Camillo escorted

Florizel and Perdita back to Sicilia, taking as much care 'as if The scene you play were mine', and finding ready help in Autolycus.

Throughout *Act 4* the 'machinery' that propelled the play became ever more obvious: Shakespeare seemed to want us to recognize that this is all pretence—yet at the same time to believe that it is true, and that it is all perfectly natural. The more the characters draw attention to their own existence as being merely fictional, the more we ourselves, audience and readers, begin to credit them and the action that gives them life. 'Like an old tale still . . . so like an old tale . . .' But sometimes truth is stranger than fiction.

When the play's final scene opens, we are with Leontes and those who have followed Paulina to the exhibition of the statue—and *nobody*, even those who have read the source story, knows what is going to happen. We can identify with Leontes, fixing our gaze so intently that we almost breathe life back into Hermione—we *will* her to come back to Leontes and to us! It is not simply that we all like the story to have a happy ending. Shakespeare, through his verse and stagecraft, manipulates the audience/readers into an indulgence of some of the deepest human longings—to undo what has been done, to recover what has been lost, to avoid the inevitable consequences of our actions, and to be granted forgiveness for all the sins we have committed.

Providing a larger overview through the Chorus, the play seems to assure us that, in the fullness of Time, all will indeed be well: there will be a happy issue out of all afflictions. This is the way the imagery has been working too, imperceptibly and even subliminally. We have been persuaded to accept the rhythm of the seasons, of winter followed by spring, 'middle summer' (4, 4, 107) and then the ripe fruition of autumn. The 'branch' of the first scene at last bears fruit. Time the destroyer is also Time the healer and creator, bringing new life to the dead land when spring, in the person of Perdita (who has been fleetingly compared with Proserpina—4, 4, 116), is returned to Sicilia, the country of her birth, and to her mother.

Perhaps the ending of *The Winter's Tale* is fantastic—but don't we all wish things were like that. And perhaps they are . . . ?

Source, Date, and Text

Shakespeare's source for this play was *Pandosto*, a prose romance by Robert Greene which was first published in 1588 and reprinted many times before *The Winter's Tale* was written—probably between 1 January and 15 May 1611. The earlier of these dates is suggested by a reference within the play itself when one of the groups in the 'satyr' dance of *Act 4*, Scene 4 is said to have 'danced before the king': Ben Jonson's *Masque of Oberon*, performed at court on 1 January 1611, features similar dancing 'satyrs'. The later date is fixed by an entry in the diary of Simon Forman, a quack doctor and astrologer, who records the performance he saw at the Globe theatre. His account of the action is detailed and (on the whole) accurate, but the greatest impression was made by Autolycus, 'the Rog that cam in all tottered like a coll pixie', prompting Forman to remind himself to 'beware of trusting feigned beggars or fawninge fellouss'.

The Winter's Tale was not published until 1623, in the First Folio collection of Shakespeare's plays. The present edition makes use of the text established by Ernest Schanzer (The New Penguin Shakespeare, 1969).

Shakespeare's Verse

Shakespeare's plays are written mainly in 'blank verse', the form preferred by most dramatists in the sixteenth and early seventeenth centuries. It is a very flexible medium, which is capable—like the human speaking voice—of a wide range of tones. Basically the lines, which are unrhymed, are ten syllables long. The syllables have alternating stresses, just like normal English speech; and they divide into five 'feet'. The technical name for this is 'iambic pentameter'.

At the beginning of his career Shakespeare wrote more regular, 'end-stopped', lines, where a grammatical unit of meaning could be contained within each verse line—as in Polixenes' praise of his son, 'He makes a July's day short as December' (*1, 2, 169*). Now, in *The Winter's Tale*, Shakespeare's complete mastery of his craft enables him to write a silky, fluid verse in which the thought runs effortlessly between the lines:

> **Polixenes**
> Nine chánges óf the wátery stár hath béen
> The shépherd's nóte since wé have léft our thróne
> Withóut a búrden. Tíme as lóng agáin
> Would bé fill'd úp, my bróther, wíth our thánks,
> And yét we shóuld for pérpetúitý
> Go hénce in débt. And thérefore, líke a cípher
> Yet stánding ín rich pláce, I múltiplý
> With óne 'We thánk you' mány thóusands móre
> That gó befóre it.
> **Leontes**
>   Stáy your thánks a whíle,
> And páy them whén you párt.
> **Polixenes**
>   Sir, thát's tomórrow.
> I am quéstion'd bý my féars of whát may chánce
> Or bréed upón our ábsence. Thát may blów
> No snéaping wínds at hóme, to máke us sáy
> 'This ís put fórth too trúly'! Besídes, I have stáy'd
> To tíre your róyalty.

Leontes
>   We are tóugher, bróther,
> Than yóu can pút us tó't.

Polixenes
>   No lónger stáy.

Leontes
> One sév'n-night lónger.

Polixenes
>   Véry sóoth, tomórrow.

(1, 2, 1–17)

Polixenes initiates the rhythm, and then—as in a musical duet—Leontes joins in. Sharing the pentameters between them, their courtly decorum is emphasized by the formal rhythm—and the rhythm itself is validated by their courtesy. But the harmony thus established is broken soon afterwards when Leontes, his emotions in turmoil, voices his confused thoughts to himself—in the hearing of the audience:

Leontes
> Inch-thíck, knee-déep, o'er héad and eárs a fórk'd one!
> Go pláy, boy, pláy: thy móther pláys, and Í
> Play tóo—but só disgrác'd a párt, whose íssue
> Will híss me tó my gráve. Contémpt and clámour
> Will bé my knéll. Go pláy, boy, pláy. There háve been,
> Or Í am múch decéiv'd, cuckólds ere nów . . .

(1, 1, 186–91)

The stresses of the lines are changed—and changeable! So firmly has the iambic mode been fixed by now (for actors and audience alike) that individual variations are possible without disrupting the base rhythm.

Leontes' soliloquizing also turns into a 'duet'—but soon the speakers sharing the pentameter are at odds with each other, and more like tennis-players than singers:

Camillo
>   Goód my lórd, be cúr'd
> Of thís diséas'd opínion, ánd betímes,
> For 'tís most dángeróus.

Leontes
>   Say ít be, 'tis trúe.

Camillo
No, nó, my lórd!

(I, I, 296–9)

The strong pentameter allows for a speedy exchange between the two, keeping the ground rhythm ever constant.

Characters in the Play

Time: the Chorus

SICILIA

Leontes	*king of Sicilia*
Hermione	*his wife*
Mamillius	*his son*
Perdita	*his daughter*
Camillo **Antigonus** **Cleomenes** **Dion**	*lords at the court of* Leontes
Paulina	*wife of* Antigonus
Emilia	*a lady attending on* Hermione
Gaoler	
Mariner	

Other Lords and Gentlemen, Ladies, Officers, and Servants at the court of Leontes

BOHEMIA

Polixenes	*king of Bohemia*
Florizel	*his son*
Archidamus	*a lord at the court of* Polixenes
Autolycus	*a rogue*
Shepherd	*supposed father of* Perdita
Clown	*his son*
Mopsa **Dorcas**	*shepherdesses*
Servant	*in the* Shepherd's *household*

Twelve countrymen, disguised as satyrs

Other Shepherds and Shepherdesses

Act 1

Act 1   Scene 1

Two courtiers exchange compliments,
speaking in an elegant, formal prose. Their
conversation allows the audience to learn
about the close relationship of two
monarchs, and of the very special esteem in
which the king's son is held.

2 *the like*: a similar.
   on foot: engaged.

8 *entertainment*: hospitality.
9 *justified in*: excused (for the unworthy
   entertainment) by.

11 *Verily*: in truth.
    I speak . . . knowledge: I am speaking
    what I know to be true.
13 *sleepy*: sleep-inducing.
14 *unintelligent*: unconscious, unaware.
    insufficience: deficiencies.

19–20 *as . . . utterance*: I know what I am
       saying, and I must say it in all fairness
       to you.
21 *Sicilia . . . Bohemia*: the king of Sicilia
    (Leontes) . . . the king of Bohemia
    (Polixenes).
22 *trained*: brought up, raised; the
    horticultural sense of 'trained' produces
    the other gardening metaphors in the
    sentence.

Scene 1

Enter Camillo *and* Archidamus

Archidamus
If you shall chance, Camillo, to visit Bohemia, on the
like occasion whereon my services are now on foot,
you shall see, as I have said, great difference betwixt
our Bohemia and your Sicilia.

Camillo
5 I think this coming summer the king of Sicilia
means to pay Bohemia the visitation which he justly
owes him.

Archidamus
Wherein our entertainment shall shame us: we will
be justified in our loves. For indeed—

Camillo
10 Beseech you—

Archidamus
Verily, I speak it in the freedom of my knowledge:
we cannot with such magnificence, in so rare—I
know not what to say. We will give you sleepy drinks,
that your senses, unintelligent of our insufficience,
15 may, though they cannot praise us, as little accuse
us.

Camillo
You pay a great deal too dear for what's given
freely.

Archidamus
Believe me, I speak as my understanding instructs
20 me and as mine honesty puts it to utterance.

Camillo
Sicilia cannot show himself over-kind to Bohemia.
They were trained together in their childhoods; and

24 *choose*: help, avoid.
   branch: flourish, put out branches; *and also* diverge, separate.
25 *mature dignities*: high positions in adult life.
   necessities: obligations.
26 *encounters*: meetings, intercourse.
27 *royally attorneyed*: carried out magnificently by their deputies.
30 *vast*: void, a wide expanse of space or time.
30–1 *from . . . winds*: from all corners of the earth.
31 *The . . . loves*: long may their love last.

there rooted betwixt them then such an affection, which cannot choose but branch now. Since their more
25 mature dignities and royal necessities made separation of their society, their encounters, though not personal, hath been royally attorneyed with interchange of gifts, letters, loving embassies: that they have seemed to be together, though absent; shook hands as over a
30 vast; and embraced, as it were, from the ends of opposed winds. The heavens continue their loves!

Archidamus
I think there is not in the world either malice or matter to alter it. You have an unspeakable comfort of your young prince Mamillius. It is a gentleman of
35 the greatest promise that ever came into my note.
Camillo
I very well agree with you in the hopes of him. It is a gallant child; one that indeed physics the subject, makes old hearts fresh. They that went on crutches ere he was born desire yet their life to see him a man.
Archidamus
40 Would they else be content to die?
Camillo
Yes—if there were no other excuse why they should desire to live.
Archidamus
If the king had no son, they would desire to live on crutches till he had one.

[*Exeunt*

33 *matter*: reason, substance.

37 *physics the subject*: is a tonic for everybody in the land.
38–9 *They that . . . a man*: those who were old even before he was born want to go on living until he is grown up.
40 *else*: otherwise.

Act 1   Scene 2

This important scene, which is all in verse, runs the gamut of emotions from easy, relaxed gaiety to tense suspicion and murderous jealousy. Leontes urges his companion—the friend he has known from childhood—to stay with him just a little longer. At first Polixenes is adamant, but eventually he yields to persuasion from Hermione, the wife of Leontes. Such yielding, however, generates alarm in the mind of Leontes and he begins to distrust his wife, voicing his thoughts aloud to himself (in the hearing of the audience) and then to his trusted counsellor, Camillo. Camillo promises to take some action, and the king is satisfied—but Camillo gives a warning to Polixenes (who has already noticed a change in Leontes' behaviour). The king of Bohemia plans an immediate departure from Sicilia, taking Camillo with him.

1–2 *Nine . . . note*: the shepherd has recorded the passage of nine months by observing the phases of the moon (called 'the watery star' because of its connection with the movement of tides).

3 *burden*: occupant (*and also* the refrain of the shepherd's song).

5–6 *for . . . debt*: be eternally grateful to you when we leave.

6 *like a cipher*: like the figure 'o' (when this is added to 1,000, for example, it makes 10,000).

9 *Stay*: delay, postpone.

11 *question'd*: worried.

11–12 *chance . . . absence*: happen or develop because I am away from home (Polixenes uses the 'royal plural').

12–14 *That . . . truly*: that would cause enough serious trouble to make me realize that I had been right to worry.

13 *sneaping*: biting.

15 *royalty*: majesty.

15–16 *We are . . . to't*: I can take more of that than you can try me with. Leontes, also using the 'royal plural', addresses Polixenes with affection as a brother king.

17 *sev'n-night*: week.
 Very sooth: really and truly.

18 *part*: split.

Scene 2

Enter Leontes, Hermione, Mamillius, Polixenes, Camillo, *and* Attendants

Polixenes
Nine changes of the watery star hath been
The shepherd's note since we have left our throne
Without a burden. Time as long again
Would be fill'd up, my brother, with our thanks,
5 And yet we should for perpetuity
Go hence in debt. And therefore, like a cipher
Yet standing in rich place, I multiply
With one 'We thank you' many thousands more
That go before it.

Leontes
                    Stay your thanks a while,
10 And pay them when you part.

Polixenes
                              Sir, that's tomorrow.
I am question'd by my fears of what may chance
Or breed upon our absence. That may blow
No sneaping winds at home, to make us say
'This is put forth too truly'! Besides, I have stay'd
15 To tire your royalty.

Leontes
                        We are tougher, brother,
Than you can put us to't.

Polixenes
                          No longer stay.

Leontes
One sev'n-night longer.

Polixenes
                        Very sooth, tomorrow.

Leontes
We'll part the time between's then; and in that
I'll no gainsaying.

Polixenes
                    Press me not, beseech you so.
20 There is no tongue that moves, none, none i'th'world,
So soon as yours could win me. So it should now,
Were there necessity in your request, although
'Twere needful I denied it. My affairs
Do even drag me homeward; which to hinder

19 *I'll no gainsaying*: I will not be refused.
   so: in such a way.
20 *moves*: persuades.
21–3 *So it . . . denied it*: it would persuade
   me now if you were asking for
   something you really needed, however
   much—in my own interests—I ought to
   refuse it.
25 *Were . . . to me*: would cause me pain,
   even though you did it for love.
28–9 *drawn oaths*: made him swear.

31–2 *this . . . proclaim'd*: yesterday's news
   told us that all was well.

33 *ward*: defensive posture (a term of
   fencing).
34 *To tell . . . strong*: to say that he is
   longing to see his son would make a
   good argument (for going home).
35 *But*: only.
37 *We'll . . . distaffs*: we women will drive
   him away. The distaff (used in spinning
   wool) was a symbol of womanhood.
38 *adventure*: risk.
39 *borrow of*: loan for.
40 *take*: keep, receive.
   give . . . commission: authorize him.
41 *let him*: allow him (to stay).
41–2 *behind . . . parting*: later than the time
   pre-arranged for his departure (*gest* =
   stage or halt in a royal progress).
42 *good deed*: indeed.
43 *jar*: tick.
44 *What . . . lord*: any woman anywhere
   can love her husband.
45 *verily*: indeed.
47 *limber*: feeble, flimsy.
48 *unsphere the stars*: shake the stars out of
   their normal courses.
50 *A lady's 'verily' is*: a lady's use of the
   oath 'verily' is.

25 Were, in your love, a whip to me, my stay
   To you a charge and trouble. To save both,
   Farewell, our brother.
   Leontes
                     Tongue-tied, our queen? Speak you.
   Hermione
   I had thought, sir, to have held my peace until
   You had drawn oaths from him not to stay. You, sir,
30 Charge him too coldly. Tell him you are sure
   All in Bohemia's well: this satisfaction
   The by-gone day proclaim'd. Say this to him,
   He's beat from his best ward.
   Leontes
                             Well said, Hermione.
   Hermione
   To tell he longs to see his son were strong.
35 But let him say so, then, and let him go;
   But let him swear so and he shall not stay:
   We'll thwack him hence with distaffs.

           Leontes *draws apart*

   Yet of your royal presence I'll adventure
   The borrow of a week. When at Bohemia
40 You take my lord, I'll give him my commission
   To let him there a month behind the gest
   Prefix'd for's parting; yet, good deed, Leontes,
   I love thee not a jar o'th'clock behind
   What lady she her lord. You'll stay?
   Polixenes
                                 No, madam.
   Hermione
45 Nay, but you will!
   Polixenes
                 I may not, verily.
   Hermione
   Verily!
   You put me off with limber vows; but I,
   Though you would seek t'unsphere the stars with
     oaths,
   Should yet say, 'Sir, no going'. Verily,
50 You shall not go. A lady's 'verily' is
   As potent as a lord's. Will you go yet?

53 *pay your fees*: In Shakespeare's time it was usual to make released prisoners pay a fee to the gaoler (even if they had been wrongfully arrested).

57 *import offending*: imply that I have committed an offence.

62 *pretty lordings*: fine young gentlemen.

63 *no more behind*: nothing more (to worry about).
65 *boy eternal*: boys for ever.

66 *verier wag*: more of a rascal.

67 *twinn'd*: identical.
68 *chang'd*: exchanged, gave each other.
70 *The doctrine of ill-doing*: how to do wrong.
72–3 *our . . . blood*: our youthful innocence had not developed into physical maturity.
73–5 *answered . . . ours*: on the Day of Judgement we would be able to declare ourselves innocent of all personal sin—provided that we were set free from the guilt of 'original sin' (which every human being inherits in descending from Adam).
75 *gather*: deduce, infer.

76 *tripp'd since*: done something wrong since then.
77 *born to's*: presented to us.
78 *unfledg'd days*: days when we were 'nestlings' (= young birds without feathers).

Force me to keep you as a prisoner,
Not like a guest; so you shall pay your fees
When you depart, and save your thanks. How say you?
55 My prisoner? Or my guest? By your dread 'verily',
One of them you shall be.
    Polixenes
                           Your guest, then, madam:
To be your prisoner should import offending;
Which is for me less easy to commit
Than you to punish.
    Hermione
                  Not your gaoler, then,
60 But your kind hostess. Come, I'll question you
Of my lord's tricks, and yours, when you were boys.
You were pretty lordings then?
    Polixenes
                      We were, fair queen,
Two lads that thought there was no more behind
But such a day tomorrow as today,
65 And to be boy eternal.
    Hermione
                 Was not my lord
The verier wag o'th'two?
    Polixenes
We were as twinn'd lambs that did frisk i'th'sun,
And bleat the one at th'other. What we chang'd
Was innocence for innocence: we knew not
70 The doctrine of ill-doing, nor dream'd
That any did. Had we pursu'd that life,
And our weak spirits ne'er been higher rear'd
With stronger blood, we should have answer'd heaven
Boldly 'Not guilty', the imposition cleared
75 Hereditary ours.
    Hermione
              By this we gather
You have tripp'd since.
    Polixenes
             O my most sacred lady,
Temptations have since then been born to's: for
In those unfledg'd days was my wife a girl;

79   *cross'd the eyes*: been seen by.
80   *Grace to boot!*: Heaven help us—i.e.
     whatever will you say next!

81   *Of this . . . conclusion*: don't go on with
     that argument.

84–5 *that . . . that*: if . . . if.

88   *dearest*: The word is spoken as one
     syllable, 'dear'st'.
89   *To better purpose*: with a better result.

91–4 *Cram's . . . make's . . . ride's*: This
     unusual use of the apostrophe ('cram us
     . . .', etc.) marks a change in
     Hermione's tones from the formal and
     courtly to the closely intimate.
92–3 *one . . . upon that*: if one good deed is
     not praised, then many others—which
     would have been inspired by that
     praise—will not be performed.
94–6 *You . . . acre*: i.e. you will get a lot
     more out of us [women] with kindness
     than with harsh treatment.
96   *heat an acre*: gallop a furlong.
     goal: point.
98   *an elder sister*: an earlier one that is just
     the same.
99   *I would . . . Grace*: I wish the other good
     deed had been such as to win me grace
     and favour.
101 *I long*: I long to hear it.
102 *crabbed*: bitter (like crab-apples).
103 *Ere*: before.
104 *clap . . . love*: agree—by shaking
     hands—to be my wife.

Your precious self had then not cross'd the eyes
80 Of my young playfellow.
     Hermione
                         Grace to boot!
Of this make no conclusion, lest you say
Your queen and I are devils. Yet go on:
Th'offences we have made you do we'll answer,
If you first sinn'd with us, and that with us
85 You did continue fault, and that you slipp'd not
With any but with us.
     Leontes [*Approaching*] Is he won yet?
     Hermione
He'll stay, my lord.
     Leontes
                    At my request he would not.
Hermione, my dearest, thou never spok'st
To better purpose.
     Hermione
                  Never?
     Leontes
                        Never but once.
     Hermione
90 What? Have I twice said well? When was't before?
I prithee tell me. Cram's with praise, and make's
As fat as tame things. One good deed dying
     tongueless
Slaughters a thousand waiting upon that.
Our praises are our wages. You may ride's
95 With one soft kiss a thousand furlongs ere
With spur we heat an acre. But to th'goal:
My last good deed was to entreat his stay.
What was my first? It has an elder sister,
Or I mistake you. O, would her name were Grace!
100 But once before I spoke to th'purpose? When?
Nay, let me have't; I long.
     Leontes
                          Why, that was when
Three crabbed months had soured themselves to
     death
Ere I could make thee open thy white hand
And clap thyself my love: then didst thou utter
105 'I am yours for ever'.

105 *'Tis Grace indeed*: i.e. the earlier good
    deed did certainly win grace and favour
    for Hermione.
106 *lo you now*: just look at that.
109 *To . . . far*: to take friendship too far.
    mingling bloods: In early (Aristotelian)
    physiology, sexual intercourse was
    thought of as a mingling of the bloods
    of the lovers.
110 *tremor cordis*: fluttering of the heart.
    dances: The usual expression is 'dances
    for joy'—but Leontes contradicts this.
111 *entertainment*: hospitality.
112–14 *May . . . agent*: may look innocent,
    be freely given in all sincerity,
    generosity, warm-heartedness, and be a
    credit to the one who offers it.
114 *'t may, I grant*: I agree that this may be
    so.
115 *paddling palms*: fingering each other's
    hands.
117–18 *to sigh . . . deer*: to give sighs that
    sound like the noise made by a hunting-
    horn when it signals the death of the
    deer.
119 *brows*: forehead: Leontes refers to the
    popular jest that horns would sprout on
    the head of a cuckold (= a man whose
    wife is unfaithful to him).

120 *I'fecks*: in faith. The disturbance in
    Leontes' mind is signalled by changes
    in vocabulary, syntax, and speech-
    rhythms.
121 *bawcock*: fine chap.
    smutch'd: smudged, dirtied.
123 *neat*: tidy; but Leontes immediately
    corrects himself as he recollects that
    'neat' is a term for 'horned cattle'.

Hermione

            'Tis Grace indeed.
Why, lo you now, I have spoke to th'purpose twice:
The one for ever earn'd a royal husband;
Th'other for some while a friend.

She gives her hand to Polixenes

Leontes [*Aside*]

                        Too hot, too hot!
To mingle friendship far is mingling bloods.
110 I have *tremor cordis* on me: my heart dances,
But not for joy, not joy. This entertainment
May a free face put on, derive a liberty
From heartiness, from bounty, fertile bosom,
And well become the agent—'t may, I grant.
115 But to be paddling palms and pinching fingers,
As now they are, and making practis'd smiles
As in a looking glass; and then to sigh, as 'twere
The mort o'th'deer—O, that is entertainment
My bosom likes not, nor my brows! Mamillius,

Mamillius *comes forward*

120 Art thou my boy?
        Mamillius

                Ay, my good lord.
        Leontes

                        I'fecks!
Why, that's my bawcock. What, hast smutch'd thy
    nose?
They say it is a copy out of mine. Come, captain,
We must be neat—not neat but cleanly, captain.
And yet the steer, the heifer, and the calf

125 *virginalling*: playing with her fingers
    upon the virginals (see illustration);
    there is also a subdued play on 'virgin'
    or 'virginal'.
126 *wanton*: playful, naughty.
128 *Thou . . . have*: you need a hairy head
    and the bull's horns that I am
    sprouting.

129 *full*: completely.
130 *as like as eggs*: A proverbial saying.
132 *o'er-dy'd blacks*: mourning clothes that
    have been dyed over into—or from—
    another colour.
133-4 *As . . . mine*: as the dice used by a
    cheating gambler who ignores the rules.
134 *bourn*: boundary.
136 *welkin*: blue as the sky.
137 *My collop*: piece of my flesh.
    dam: mother.
138 *Affection*: sexual desire. From this point,
    Leontes' thought-processes become
    very involved—but the general direction
    is clear.
    intention: fervour, intensity.
    centre: heart of the matter.
139 *not so held*: thought not to be possible.
140 *Communicat'st with dreams*: are related
    to things we only dream about.
141-2 *With . . . nothing*: work with what is
    not real, and make something out of
    nothing.
142 *very credent*: easily believable.
143 *co-join with something*: latch on to
    something that is real.
    and thou dost: and that is what is
    happening.
144 *beyond commission*: more than could be
    expected.
145-6 *to the . . . brows*: with the result that
    my mind is infected and my forehead
    begins to sprout horns.
146 *What means Sicilia*: what is wrong with
    Leontes.
147 *something seems unsettled*: seems rather
    disturbed.
148 *How is't with you*: are you feeling all
    right.

125 Are all called neat. Still virginalling
    Upon his palm?—How now, you wanton calf!
    Art thou my calf?

Mamillius
                    Yes, if you will, my lord.
     Leontes
     Thou want'st a rough pash and the shoots that I have
     To be full like me; yet they say we are
130 Almost as like as eggs. Women say so,
     That will say anything. But were they false
     As o'er-dy'd blacks, as wind, as waters, false
     As dice are to be wish'd by one that fixes
     No bourn 'twixt his and mine, yet were it true
135 To say this boy were like me. Come, sir page,
     Look on me with your welkin eye. Sweet villain!
     Most dear'st! My collop! Can thy dam? May't be?
     Affection, thy intention stabs the centre.
     Thou dost make possible things not so held,
140 Communicat'st with dreams—how can this be?—
     With what's unreal thou coactive art,
     And fellow'st nothing. Then 'tis very credent
     Thou mayst co-join with something; and thou dost,
     And that beyond commission, and I find it,
145 And that to the infection of my brains
     And hardening of my brows.
          Polixenes
                              What means Sicilia?
          Hermione
     He something seems unsettled.
          Polixenes
                                  How, my lord!
     What cheer? How is't with you, best brother?

Hermione

You look
As if you held a brow of much distraction.
150 Are you mov'd, my lord?

Leontes

No, in good earnest.
How sometimes Nature will betray its folly,
Its tenderness, and make itself a pastime
To harder bosoms! Looking on the lines
Of my boy's face, methoughts I did recoil
155 Twenty-three years, and saw myself unbreech'd,
In my green velvet coat; my dagger muzzl'd,
Lest it should bite its master and so prove,
As ornaments oft does, too dangerous.
How like, methought, I then was to this kernel,
160 This squash, this gentleman. Mine honest friend,
Will you take eggs for money?

Mamillius

No, my lord, I'll fight.

Leontes

You will? Why, happy man be's dole! My brother,
Are you so fond of your young prince as we
165 Do seem to be of ours?

Polixenes

If at home, sir,
He's all my exercise, my mirth, my matter;
Now my sworn friend, and then mine enemy;
My parasite, my soldier, statesman, all.
He makes a July's day short as December,
170 And with his varying childness cures in me
Thoughts that would thick my blood.

Leontes

So stands this squire
Offic'd with me. We two will walk, my lord,
And leave you to your graver steps. Hermione,
How thou lov'st us show in our brother's welcome.
175 Let what is dear in Sicily be cheap.
Next to thyself and my young rover, he's
Apparent to my heart.

Hermione

If you would seek us,
We are yours i'th'garden. Shall's attend you there?

149 *held . . . distraction*: have a lot on your mind.
150 *mov'd*: angry about something.
in good earnest: quite honestly.
151-2 *betray . . . tenderness*: show itself to be silly and sentimental.
152 *pastime*: laughing-stock.
153 *lines*: lineaments.
154 *methoughts . . . recoil*: I thought that I went back; the remark seems to establish Leontes' age at around 30.
155 *unbreech'd*: not yet in breeches, still wearing a dress.

156 *muzzl'd*: sheathed, protected.
160 *squash*: unripe pea-pod (= youngster).
161 *take eggs for money*: be paid with something cheap instead of money; a proverbial saying.
163 *happy . . . dole*: good luck to you (a proverbial expression meaning 'may his lot in life be that of a happy man').
165 *If at home*: when I am at home.
166 *He's . . . matter*: he keeps me busy, makes me laugh, and is all I talk about.
168 *parasite*: favourite.
169 *December*: i.e. a day in December.
170 *varying childness*: childish whims.
171 *thick my blood*: depress me, cause melancholy.
171-2 *So . . . me*: this young man does the same for me.
172 *We two*: i.e. Leontes and Mamillius.
173 *graver*: slower, more serious.
175 *dear*: expensive—and also beloved.
177 *Apparent*: heir apparent, the person most close.
178 *Shall's attend*: shall we wait for you.

179 *To . . . you*: do whatever you please.
     found: discovered, found out.
180 *Be you*: wherever you are.
181 *give line*: An angler lets out his line
     before pulling in the fish that he has
     caught.
183 *neb*: beak, mouth.
184 *arms her*: takes his arm.
185 *allowing*: permissive, complaisant.
     Gone: (a) departed; (b) lost to Leontes;
     (c) fallen into sin.
186 *Inch-thick*: solid proof (as firm as an
     inch-thick plank).
     knee-deep: i.e. deep in sin.
     o'er . . . one: completely cuckolded (see
     line 119 *note*).
187–8 *Go play . . . Play too*: Leontes himself
     plays with the word. His child is sent
     away to amuse himself, whilst his
     mother is enjoying herself with a lover
     and Leontes must perform the role of a
     husband whose wife is unfaithful.
188 *disgrac'd*: disgraceful.
     issue: outcome, catastrophe.
189 *hiss*: The 'actor' playing the part of the
     cuckold will be hissed off the stage by
     the audience.
190 *my knell*: the death of me.
191 *ere*: before.
192 *even at this present*: right now; Leontes
     seems to appeal to the audience.
194 *sluic'd*: violated, ravished; the metaphor
     of drawing off water from a pond
     introduces a chain of metaphors in the
     succeeding lines.
196 *Sir Smile*: the smiling gentleman;
     Shakespeare often associates deceit and
     villainy with smiles.
     comfort in't: some consolation (to know
     that I am not the only one).
197 *Whiles*: so long as.
199 *revolted*: unfaithful.
200 *Physic . . . none*: there is no cure for this
     condition.
201–2 *It is . . . predominant*: the infidelity of
     wives will take advantage of every
     opportunity—just like a planet whose
     destructive influence will be felt
     whenever it is in the ascendant.
202 *think it*: believe me.
204 *No barricado . . . belly*: there is no way
     of barricading a woman's womb.
     Know't: you can be sure of it.
206 *bag and baggage*: everything there is.
     on's: of us.

Leontes
To your own bents dispose you: you'll be found,
180 Be you beneath the sky. [*Aside*] I am angling now,
Though you perceive me not how I give line.
Go to, go to!
How she holds up the neb, the bill to him!
And arms her with the boldness of a wife
185 To her allowing husband!
            [*Exeunt* Hermione *and* Polixenes
                              Gone already!
Inch-thick, knee-deep, o'er head and ears a fork'd
   one!
Go play, boy, play: thy mother plays, and I
Play too—but so disgrac'd a part, whose issue
Will hiss me to my grave. Contempt and clamour
190 Will be my knell. Go play, boy, play. There have
   been,
Or I am much deceiv'd, cuckolds ere now;
And many a man there is, even at this present,
Now, while I speak this, holds his wife by th'arm,
That little thinks she has been sluic'd in's absence,
195 And his pond fish'd by his next neighbour, by
Sir Smile, his neighbour. Nay, there's comfort in't
Whiles other men have gates, and those gates
   open'd,
As mine, against their will. Should all despair
That have revolted wives, the tenth of mankind
200 Would hang themselves. Physic for't there's none:
It is a bawdy planet, that will strike
Where 'tis predominant; and 'tis powerful, think it,
From east, west, north, and south. Be it concluded,
No barricado for a belly. Know't:
205 It will let in and out the enemy
With bag and baggage. Many thousand on's
Have the disease and feel't not. How now, boy?
     Mamillius
I am like you, they say.
     Leontes
                         Why, that's some comfort.
What! Camillo there!
     Camillo
210 Ay, my good lord.

He comes forward

Leontes

Go play, Mamillius. Thou'rt an honest man.

                [*Exit* Mamillius

Camillo, this great sir will yet stay longer.

Camillo

You had much ado to make his anchor hold:

When you cast out, it still came home.

Leontes

                         Didst note it?

Camillo

213 *make . . . hold*: keep him here.

214 *still came home*: always came back.

215 He would not stay at your petitions, made

His business more material.

Leontes

                   Didst perceive it?

[*Aside*] They're here with me already: whispering,

   rounding,

'Sicilia is a so-forth'. 'Tis far gone

When I shall gust it last.—How came't Camillo,

220 That he did stay?

Camillo

               At the good queen's entreaty.

Leontes

'At the queen's', be't. 'Good' should be pertinent;

But, so it is, it is not. Was this taken

By any understanding pate but thine?

For thy conceit is soaking, will draw in

225 More than the common blocks. Not noted, is't,

But of the finer natures? By some severals

Of headpiece extraordinary? Lower messes

Perchance are to this business purblind? Say.

Camillo

Business, my lord? I think most understand

230 Bohemia stays here longer.

Leontes

                     Ha?

Camillo

                    Stays here longer.

Leontes

Ay, but why?

Camillo

To satisfy your highness, and the entreaties

Of our most gracious mistress.

215–16 *made . . . material*: argued that his work was more important.

217 *They're . . . already*: people can already see what's going on.
rounding: whispering in corners.

218 *so-forth*: so-and-so; Leontes winces away from the word 'cuckold'.

219 *gust*: get to hear, perceive.
cam't: did it come about.

222 *so it is*: as it happens.
taken: understood.

223 *pate*: brain.

224–5 *thy conceit . . . blocks*: your intelligence soaks things up and absorbs them more quickly than ordinary blockheads.

225–7 *Not noted . . . extraordinary*: it hasn't been noticed, has it, except by the more sensitive people—by those individuals who are more perceptive than most.

227 *lower messes*: the lower classes (a 'mess' = a group of people served together at table).

228 *Perchance*: perhaps.
business: Leontes picks up Camillo's innocent word from line 216 and gives it sexual emphasis.
purblind: quite blind.

233 *Satisfy*: Leontes is developing the sexual sense of the word.

236 *nearest*: most intimate.
237 *chamber-counsels*: private, confidential
    conversations.
237-9 *wherein . . . reform'd*: Camillo has
    acted as a father-confessor to Leontes,
    listening to his innermost thoughts (the
    thoughts of his 'bosom').
241 *seems so*: i.e. which only seems to be
    genuine.
242 *bide upon't*: dwell more on the subject.
243-5 *If thou . . . require'd*: even if you want to
    be honest, you are a coward—and your
    cowardice undercuts your honesty,
    preventing it from doing what needs to
    be done. Leontes arrives at the
    metaphor 'hoxes . . . behind' (= laming
    cattle by cutting the hamstrings) from
    the association of *coward* with *cowherd*.
245-7 *Or else . . . or else*: either . . . or.
245 *counted*: considered.
246 *grafted*: grown in (like a shoot in a host
    plant).

248 *a game . . . drawn*: a gamble played
    through to the end with a rich prize for
    the winner.
249 *all for jest*: just as a joke.
251 *free*: guiltless.
253 *infinite doings*: everything that is
    happening.
254 *Sometime puts forth*: will come out at
    some time.
255 *wilful-negligent*: knowingly careless.
256 *industriously*: intentionally.
258 *weighing . . . end*: thinking carefully
    about the effects.
259 *issue*: outcome.
260-1 *Whereof . . . performance*: although the
    unperformed task was crying out to be
    done.
263 *allow'd infirmities*: excusable weaknesses.
265-6 *let . . . visage*: tell me what I have
    done wrong by showing me what my
    mistake looks like.

Leontes

                                Satisfy?
Th'entreaties of your mistress? Satisfy?
235 Let that suffice. I have trusted thee, Camillo,
With all the nearest things to my heart, as well
My chamber-counsels, wherein, priestlike, thou
Hast cleans'd my bosom, I from thee departed
Thy penitent reform'd. But we have been
240 Deceiv'd in thy integrity, deceiv'd
In that which seems so.

Camillo

                        Be it forbid, my lord!

Leontes

To bide upon't: thou art not honest; or
If thou inclin'st that way, thou art a coward,
Which hoxes honesty behind, restraining
245 From course requir'd. Or else thou must be counted
A servant grafted in my serious trust
And therein negligent, or else a fool
That see'st a game play'd home, the rich stake
      drawn,
And tak'st it all for jest.

Camillo

                        My gracious lord,
250 I may be negligent, foolish, and fearful:
In every one of these no man is free,
But that his negligence, his folly, fear,
Among the infinite doings of the world,
Sometime puts forth. In your affairs, my lord,
255 If ever I were wilful-negligent,
It was my folly; if industriously
I play'd the fool, it was my negligence,
Not weighing well the end; if ever fearful
To do a thing where I the issue doubted,
260 Whereof the execution did cry out
Against the non-performance, 'twas a fear
Which oft infects the wisest. These, my lord,
Are such allow'd infirmities that honesty
Is never free of. But, beseech your grace,
265 Be plainer with me, let me know my trespass
By its own visage; if I then deny it,
'Tis none of mine.

Leontes

267 *Ha'*: have.

268 *eye-glass*: eyesight (literally, lens of the eye).

270-1 *For . . . mute*: because rumour cannot keep quiet about something that can be seen so clearly.

271-2 *for cogitation . . . think*: any man capable of thinking must have thought this.

273 *slippery*: Once again, here and in the following lines, Leontes avoids using the word—'unfaithful'—that he really intends.

276 *hobby-horse*: loose woman.

277 *rank*: offensive, disgraceful.
flax-wench: peasant girl.

277-8 *puts . . . troth-plight*: goes to bed with her boyfriend before they are even legally engaged to be married (and even the troth-plight itself was not sufficient, in the eyes of the Church, for the couple to proceed to the consummation of their marriage without the religious ceremony).

280 *clouded*: doubted.

281 *present*: immediate.
'Shrew: beshrew, curse.

283-4 *which . . . true*: to repeat it would be as grave a sin as that which you accuse her of—even if that were true.

286 *stopping the career*: breaking off in the middle (in horsemanship *career* = a short gallop at full speed).

288 *Horsing foot on foot*: 'playing footsie', touching feet (e.g. under a table).

291 *pin and web*: the disease of cataract.

292 *nothing*: Leontes' fury reduces everything to nothing.

297 *betimes*: quickly.

298 *Say it be*: even if it is [dangerous].

Leontes

        Ha'not you seen, Camillo—
But that's past doubt, you have, or your eye-glass
Is thicker than a cuckold's horn—or heard—
270 For to a vision so apparent rumour
Cannot be mute—or thought—for cogitation
Resides not in that man that does not think—
My wife is slippery? If thou wilt confess—
Or else be impudently negative
275 To have nor eyes, nor ears, nor thought—then say
My wife's a hobby-horse, deserves a name
As rank as any flax-wench that puts to
Before her troth-plight: say't and justify't.

Camillo
I would not be a stander-by to hear
280 My sovereign mistress clouded so without
My present vengeance taken. 'Shrew my heart,
You never spoke what did become you less
Than this; which to reiterate were sin
As deep as that, though true.

Leontes
        Is whispering nothing?
285 Is leaning cheek to cheek? Is meeting noses?
Kissing with inside lip? Stopping the career
Of laughter with a sigh?—a note infallible
Of breaking honesty. Horsing foot on foot?
Skulking in corners? Wishing clocks more swift?
290 Hours minutes? Noon midnight? And all eyes
Blind with the pin and web but theirs, theirs only,
That would unseen be wicked,—is this nothing?
Why, then the world and all that's in't is nothing;
The covering sky is nothing; Bohemia nothing;
295 My wife is nothing; nor nothing have these nothings,
If this be nothing.

Camillo
        Good my lord, be cur'd
Of this diseas'd opinion, and betimes,
For 'tis most dangerous.

Leontes
        Say it be, 'tis true.

Camillo
No, no, my lord!

302 *hovering temporizer*: hesitating time-
    server—one who waits to see what
    answer will be most acceptable.

306 *running . . . glass*: running of sand
    through the hour-glass.

307 *like her medal*: as though she were like a
    miniature portrait of herself.

309 *bare*: carried.

310–11 'Who could see at the same time that
    what concerns my honour affects their
    own good and their own personal gain.'

312 *undo more doing*: put an end to any
    further goings-on.

313–14 *from . . . worship*: have raised from a
    humble position to one of respect (from
    a seat with the 'lower messes' (line 227)
    to a higher place at the table).

316 *gall'd*: wounded.
    bespice: add something to—i.e. poison.

317 *a lasting wink*: an everlasting sleep—i.e.
    his death.

318 'And this sleeping-draught (which is
    fatal to him) would be restorative to
    me.'

319 *rash*: hasty, quick-acting.

320 *ling'ring*: slow-acting.

321 *Maliciously*: violently.

322 *crack*: flaw, fault.

323 'Since she is so supremely honourable.'

324 *thee*: Camillo emphasizes his loving
    relationship with Leontes in the use of
    the intimate pronoun.
    Make . . . rot: if you're going to doubt
    what I say, then you can go to hell.

325 *muddy*: confused.

Leontes

         It is. You lie, you lie!

300 I say thou liest, Camillo, and I hate thee,
    Pronounce thee a gross lout, a mindless slave,
    Or else a hovering temporizer, that
    Canst with thine eyes at once see good and evil,
    Inclining to them both. Were my wife's liver

305 Infected as her life, she would not live
    The running of one glass.

Camillo

         Who does infect her?

Leontes

Why, he that wears her like her medal, hanging
About his neck, Bohemia; who, if I
Had servants true about me, that bare eyes

310 To see alike mine honour as their profits,
    Their own particular thrifts, they would do that
    Which should undo more doing. Ay, and thou,
    His cupbearer—whom I from meaner form
    Have bench'd and rear'd to worship; who mayst see

315 Plainly as heaven sees earth and earth sees heaven
    How I am gall'd—mightst bespice a cup
    To give mine enemy a lasting wink;
    Which draught to me were cordial.

Camillo

         Sir, my lord,
I could do this, and that with no rash potion,

320 But with a ling'ring dram that should not work
    Maliciously, like poison: but I cannot
    Believe this crack to be in my dread mistress,
    So sovereignly being honourable.
    I have lov'd thee—

Leontes

         Make that thy question, and go rot!

325 Dost think I am so muddy, so unsettled,
    To appoint my self in this vexation; sully
    The purity and whiteness of my sheets—
    Which to preserve is sleep, which being spotted
    Is goads, thorns, nettles, tails of wasps;

330 Give scandal to the blood o'th'prince, my son—
    Who I do think is mine, and love as mine—
    Without ripe moving to't? Would I do this?
    Could man so blench?

326 *To . . . vexation*: to put myself willingly
into this distressing situation.
327 *my sheets*: i.e. my marriage-bed.
329 *goads*: prickings.
332 *ripe moving to't*: good reason to
persuade me.
333 *blench*: delude himself.
334 *fetch . . . for't*: make away with the king
of Bohemia; Camillo's words are
carefully ambivalent.
337 *Even*: if only.
forsealing: shutting up, silencing.
338 *injury of tongues*: dangerous talk.
340 'I had intended to do just that.'

344 *keep with*: stay friends with.

347 *Account . . . servant*: never think of me
as your servant.

Camillo

                  I must believe you, sir.
I do; and will fetch off Bohemia for't:
335 Provided that when he's removed your highness
Will take again your queen as yours at first,
Even for your son's sake, and thereby forsealing
The injury of tongues in courts and kingdoms
Known and allied to yours.

Leontes

                      Thou dost advise me
340 Even so as I mine own course have set down.
I'll give no blemish to her honour, none.

Camillo

My lord,
Go then; and, with a countenance as clear
As friendship wears at feasts, keep with Bohemia
345 And with your queen. I am his cupbearer.
If from me he have wholesome beverage,
Account me not your servant.

Leontes

                  This is all.
Do't and thou hast the one half of my heart;
Do't not, thou split'st thine own.

Camillo

                    I'll do't, my lord.

Leontes

350 I will seem friendly, as thou hast advis'd me.

                                 [*Exit*

352 *case*: situation.

355–6 *in rebellion . . . so too*: because he is
rebelling against his own true self,
wants all his followers to do the same.
357 *If*: even if.

361 *forswear't*: refuse to do it.
362–3 *to . . . break-neck*: whether I do it or
not, it would certainly be the death of
me.
363 *Happy . . . now*: let's hope that this [he
sees Polixenes] will be a good sign.

Camillo

O miserable lady! But, for me,
What case stand I in? I must be the poisoner
Of good Polixenes, and my ground to do't
Is the obedience to a master—one
355 Who, in rebellion with himself, will have
All that are his so too. To do this deed,
Promotion follows. If I could find example
Of thousands that had struck anointed kings
And flourish'd after, I'd not do't; but since
360 Nor brass, nor stone, nor parchment bears not one,
Let villainy itself forswear't. I must
Forsake the court: to do't or no is certain
To me a break-neck. Happy star reign now!
Here comes Bohemia.

Enter Polixenes

Polixenes
⠀⠀⠀⠀⠀⠀⠀⠀⠀⠀⠀⠀⠀⠀⠀This is strange: methinks
365 My favour here begins to warp. Not speak?
Good day, Camillo.
⠀⠀⠀⠀**Camillo**
⠀⠀⠀⠀⠀⠀⠀⠀⠀⠀⠀⠀⠀⠀Hail, most royal sir!
Polixenes
What is the news i'th'court?
⠀⠀⠀⠀**Camillo**⠀⠀⠀⠀⠀⠀⠀⠀None rare, my lord.
Polixenes
The king hath on him such a countenance
As he had lost some province, and a region
370 Lov'd as he loves himself: even now I met him
With customary compliment, when he,
Wafting his eyes to th'contrary, and falling
A lip of much contempt, speeds from me, and
So leaves me to consider what is breeding
375 That changes thus his manners.
⠀⠀⠀⠀**Camillo**
I dare not know, my lord.
⠀⠀⠀⠀**Polixenes**
How, dare not? Do not? Do you know and dare not
Be intelligent to me? 'Tis thereabouts,
For to yourself, what you do know you must,
380 And cannot say you dare not. Good Camillo,
Your chang'd complexions are to me a mirror
Which shows me mine chang'd too: for I must be
A party in this alteration, finding
Myself thus alter'd with't.
⠀⠀⠀⠀**Camillo**
⠀⠀⠀⠀⠀⠀⠀⠀⠀⠀⠀⠀There is a sickness
385 Which puts some of us in distemper, but
I cannot name the disease; and it is caught
Of you, that yet are well.
⠀⠀⠀⠀**Polixenes**
⠀⠀⠀⠀⠀⠀⠀⠀⠀⠀⠀⠀⠀⠀How! Caught of me?
Make me not sighted like the basilisk.
I have look'd on thousands who have sped the better
390 By my regard, but killed none so. Camillo,
As you are certainly a gentleman, thereto
Clerk-like experienc'd—which no less adorns

---

365 *My . . . warp*: I seem to be losing my popularity.

370 *even now*: just this minute.

371 *compliment*: greeting.

372–3 *Wafting . . . contempt*: hurriedly turning his eyes away from me and with a contemptuous expression on his lips.

374 *breeding*: going on.

377 *How*: what do you mean.

378 *Be intelligent to me*: tell me what you know.
⠀⠀*'Tis thereabouts*: that's what it is.

379–80 *to yourself . . . not*: you can't be saying that you dare not tell yourself what it is that you know.

381–4 'When I look at the different expressions on your face, it's like looking at myself in a mirror, and I think I must be partly responsible for this alteration [in the king's attitude] since I am obviously affected by it.'

387 *Of*: from.

388 'Don't say that I look like a basilisk (= a fabulous monster whose gaze was fatal).'

389 *sped*: got on.

391–2 *thereto . . . experienc'd*: having attained that status through education.

392 *which*: i.e. education.

394 *In whose success*: by descent from whom.
 gentle: gentlemen.
395–6 *which . . . inform'd*: which it is better
 for my understanding to be told about.
397 *ignorant concealment*: concealing it to
 keep me in ignorance.

400–2 *I conjure . . . mine*: I most solemnly
 urge you, by all that is honourable in a
 man—and not the least is the obligation
 to answer my question.
403–4 *What . . . toward me*: what do you
 suspect is the likelihood of something
 harmful coming my way.
405 *if to be*: if that is possible.

407 *him*: i.e. Polixenes.

410–11 *both yourself . . . good night*: proclaim
 that we are both ruined and that's the
 end of us.

412 *him*: i.e. the man.

415–16 *As he . . . to't*: as though he had seen
 for himself, or even forced you to do it.

Our gentry than our parents' noble names,
In whose success we are gentle—I beseech you,
395 If you know aught which does behove my knowledge
Thereof to be inform'd, imprison't not
In ignorant concealment.
    Camillo
                        I may not answer.
    Polixenes
A sickness caught of me, and yet I well?
I must be answer'd. Dost thou hear, Camillo?
400 I conjure thee, by all the parts of man
Which honour does acknowledge, whereof the least
Is not this suit of mine, that thou declare
What incidency thou dost guess of harm
Is creeping toward me; how far off, how near;
405 Which way to be prevented, if to be;
If not, how best to bear it.
    Camillo
               Sir, I will tell you,
Since I am charg'd in honour, and by him
That I think honourable. Therefore mark my counsel,
Which must be ev'n as swiftly follow'd as
410 I mean to utter it, or both yourself and me
Cry lost, and so good night.
    Polixenes
             On, good Camillo.
    Camillo
I am appointed him to murder you.
    Polixenes
By whom, Camillo?
    Camillo
        By the king.
    Polixenes
           For what?
    Camillo
He thinks, nay, with all confidence he swears,
415 As he had seen't, or been an instrument
To vice you to't, that you have touch'd his queen
Forbiddenly.
    Polixenes
        O, then my best blood turn
To an infected jelly, and my name

419 *yok'd . . . Best*: linked with that of Judas
　　Iscariot who betrayed Jesus.

421 *savour*: stench.
　　dullest: least sensitive.
422 *Where I arrive*: wherever I go.

424–6 *Swear . . . influences*: however you may
　　deny his suspicions, swearing by all the
　　stars in the sky and their influences (=
　　astrological powers over human
　　destiny).
426–8 *you may . . . shake*: you might just as
　　well forbid the tides to follow the
　　changes of the moon as either remove
　　by solemn oath or change by serious
　　argument.
429–31 *The . . . body*: the crazy notion he
　　has built up from what he believes to be
　　true, and which will stay with him for
　　the rest of his life.
431 *How . . . grow*: where did this come
　　from.

435 *this trunk*: this body of mine.
436 *impawn'd*: in pawn, as a pledge.
438 *several*: different.
　　posterns: back gates.
439–41 *I'll put . . . lost*: I'll have to take my
　　chances in your service because I will
　　have no future here now that I have
　　disclosed this to you.
441 *be not uncertain*: you must not have any
　　doubts.
443–4 *which . . . stand by*: if you try to check
　　up on what I have said, I shall have to
　　deny it.
444–6 *nor shall . . . sworn*: and you yourself
　　will not be any safer than one whom the
　　king has condemned to death and
　　sworn to have executed.

448–9 *thy places . . . mine*: your position will
　　always be next to me.

Be yok'd with his that did betray the Best!
420 Turn then my freshest reputation to
A savour that may strike the dullest nostril
Where I arrive, and my approach be shunn'd,
Nay, hated too, worse than the great'st infection
That e'er was heard or read!
　　　Camillo
　　　　　　　　　　　　Swear his thought over
425 By each particular star in heaven and
By all their influences, you may as well
Forbid the sea for to obey the moon
As or by oath remove or counsel shake
The fabric of his folly, whose foundation
430 Is pil'd upon his faith, and will continue
The standing of his body.
　　　Polixenes
　　　　　　　　　　　　How should this grow?
　　　Camillo
I know not; but I am sure 'tis safer to
Avoid what's grown than question how 'tis born.
If therefore you dare trust my honesty,
435 That lies enclosed in this trunk, which you
Shall bear along impawn'd, away tonight!
Your followers I will whisper to the business,
And will by twos and threes, at several posterns,
Clear them o'th'city. For myself, I'll put
440 My fortunes to your service, which are here
By this discovery lost. Be not uncertain,
For, by the honour of my parents, I
Have utter'd truth; which if you seek to prove,
I dare not stand by; nor shall you be safer
445 Than one condemned by the king's own mouth,
　　thereon
His execution sworn.
　　　Polixenes
　　　　　　　　　　I do believe thee:
I saw his heart in's face. Give me thy hand.
Be pilot to me, and thy places shall
Still neighbour mine. My ships are ready, and
450 My people did expect my hence departure
Two days ago. This jealousy
Is for a precious creature; as she's rare
Must it be great; and as his person's mighty

Must it be violent; and as he does conceive
455 He is dishonour'd by a man which ever
Profess'd to him, why, his revenges must
In that be made more bitter. Fear o'ershades me.
Good expedition be my friend and comfort
The gracious queen, part of his theme, but nothing
460 Of his ill-ta'en suspicion! Come, Camillo,
I will respect thee as a father if
Thou bear'st my life off. Hence! Let us avoid.
Camillo
It is in mine authority to command
The keys of all the posterns. Please your highness
465 To take the urgent hour. Come, sir, away.
                                        [*Exeunt*

456 *Profess'd*: professed affection.
457 *o'ershades me*: comes over me like a cloud.
458–60 *Good expedition . . . suspicion*: may a speedy departure save me, and also be some help to the gracious queen—who must be also the object of the king's anger, although she has done nothing to justify his ill-founded suspicion.
462 *Thou . . . off*: you save my life.
Hence: away.
avoid: be gone.
464 *please*: may it please.
465 *urgent hour*: instant moment.

Act 2

Act 2   Scene 1

A quiet domestic scene is rudely interrupted
when Leontes, incensed by the discovery of
Polixenes' flight, accuses Hermione of
adultery. Antigonus is quick to speak in her
defence, but Leontes charges him with
complicity.

3 *none of you*: have nothing to do with
   you.

9 *so*: provided that.

11 *taught'*: taught you; the apostrophe
   (which is in the F text) shows that, for
   metrical reasons, a word has been
   omitted.

Scene 1

Enter Hermione, Mamillius, *and* Ladies

Hermione
Take the boy to you: he so troubles me,
'Tis past enduring.
    First Lady
                    Come, my gracious lord,
Shall I be your playfellow?
    Mamillius
                        No, I'll none of you.
    First Lady
Why, my sweet lord?
    Mamillius
5 You'll kiss me hard, and speak to me as if
I were a baby still.—I love you better.
    Second Lady
And why so, my lord?
    Mamillius
                    Not for because
Your brows are blacker; yet black brows, they say,
Become some women best, so that there be not
10 Too much hair there, but in a semicircle,
Or a half-moon, made with a pen.
    Second Lady
                        Who taught' this?
    Mamillius
I learn'd it out of women's faces. Pray now,
What colour are your eyebrows?
    First Lady
                    Blue, my lord.
    Mamillius
Nay, that's a mock. I have seen a lady's nose

15 That has been blue, but not her eyebrows.
   First Lady

                                     Hark ye:
The queen, your mother, rounds apace. We shall
Present our services to a fine new prince
One of these days; and then you'd wanton with us,
If we would have you.
   Second Lady

                        She is spread of late
20 Into a goodly bulk. Good time encounter her!
   Hermione
What wisdom stirs amongst you? Come, sir, now
I am for you again. Pray you, sit by us,
And tell's a tale.
   Mamillius

                Merry or sad shall't be?
   Hermione
As merry as you will.
   Mamillius
25 A sad tale's best for winter. I have one
Of sprites and goblins.
   Hermione

                   Let's have that, good sir.
Come on, sit down; come on, and do your best
To fright me with your sprites. You're powerful at it.
   Mamillius
There was a man—
   Hermione

               Nay, come sit down; then on.
   Mamillius
30 Dwelt by a churchyard—I will tell it softly:
Yond crickets shall not hear it.
   Hermione

                Come on, then,
And give't me in mine ear.

      Enter Leontes, Antigonus, *and* Lords

   Leontes
Was he met there? His train? Camillo with him?
   Lord
Behind the tuft of pines I met them. Never
35 Saw I men scour so on their way. I ey'd them

---

16 *apace*: fast.

17 *prince*: royal child (whether boy or girl).

18 *wanton*: play.

20 *Good . . . her*: good luck to her when she goes into labour.

22 *I am for you*: I am ready for you.

26 *sprites*: spirits, ghosts.

31 *Yond crickets*: i.e. the ladies in attendance, chattering like crickets.

32 *give't*: whisper it.

33 *train*: followers.

35 *scour*: hurry.
   ey'd: watched.

36 *Even*: all the way.

37 *my just censure*: that I made the right judgement.
38 *Alack . . . knowledge*: Oh how I wish I did not know so much.
39 *so blest*: i.e. in being right.
39–42 *in the cup . . . infected*: Leontes refers to the belief that spiders are venomous, and that anyone who drinks liquid with a spider in it will be poisoned—but only if the spider is seen.

42 *if one present*: if anyone were to show.
44 *gorge*: throat.
45 *hefts*: heavings, retching.
46 *pandar*: go-between (especially in sexual matters).
48 *All's true . . . mistrusted*: all our suspicions have been proved right.
50 *discover'd my design*: revealed my intentions.
51 *pinch'd*: tortured.
51–2 *a very . . . will*: merely a dupe for them to hoodwink as they please.
54 *no less . . . so*: done the same thing.
56 *nurse*: breast-feed.
58 *Sport*: some kind of game.
59 *about*: anywhere near.

62 *But I'd say*: it should be enough for me to say (i.e. not even swear on oath).

Even to their ships.

Leontes
                          How blest am I
In my just censure, in my true opinion!
Alack, for lesser knowledge! How accurs'd
In being so blest! There may be in the cup
40 A spider steep'd, and one may drink, depart,
And yet partake no venom, for his knowledge
Is not infected: but if one present
Th'abhorr'd ingredient to his eye, make known
How he hath drunk, he cracks his gorge, his sides,
45 With violent hefts. I have drunk, and seen the spider.
Camillo was his help in this, his pandar.
There is a plot against my life, my crown.
All's true that is mistrusted. That false villain
Whom I employ'd was pre-employ'd by him.
50 He has discover'd my design, and I
Remain a pinch'd thing; yea, a very trick
For them to play at will. How came the posterns
So easily open?

Lord
                 By his great authority;
Which often hath no less prevail'd than so
55 On your command.

Leontes
                 I know't too well.
[*To* Hermione] Give me the boy. I am glad you did
   not nurse him;
Though he does bear some signs of me, yet you
Have too much blood in him.

Hermione
                          What is this? Sport?

Leontes
Bear the boy hence; he shall not come about her.
60 Away with him, and let her sport herself
With that she's big with: for 'tis Polixenes
Has made thee swell thus.

Mamillius is led out

Hermione
                    But I'd say he had not,
And I'll be sworn you would believe my saying,

64 *lean to th'nayward*: incline to believe the opposite.

Howe'er you lean to th'nayward.
Leontes
                                    You, my lords,
65 Look on her, mark her well: be but about
   To say she is a goodly lady and
   The justice of your hearts will thereto add,
   ''Tis pity she's not honest, honourable'.

69 *without-door form*: outward appearance.
70 *speech*: praise.
   straight: immediately.
71 *petty brands*: hints of deficiency.
72 *calumny*: the voice of defamation.
   O, I am out: Oh no, I am mistaken.

   Praise her but for this her without-door form—
70 Which, on my faith, deserves high speech—and
   straight
   The shrug, the 'hum' or 'ha', these petty brands
   That calumny doth use—O, I am out!
   That mercy does, for calumny will sear
   Virtue itself—these shrugs, these 'hum's and 'ha's,
75 When you have said she's goodly, come between
   Ere you can say she's honest. But be't known,
   From him that has most cause to grieve it should be,
   She's an adult'ress.

78 *She's an adult'ress*: Leontes at last finds the words to express his thoughts.

79 *replenish'd*: complete, accomplished.
80 *as much more*: twice as much again.

   Hermione
                          Should a villain say so,
   The most replenish'd villain in the world,
80 He were as much more villain. You, my lord,
   Do but mistake.

82-3 *O . . . place*: Leontes will not call someone of her social status by the name (i.e. whore) that Hermione deserves.
84 *barbarism*: uncivilized people.
85 *a like*: the same.
   degrees: ranks of society.
86 'And forget the proper distinction that good manners makes.'

   Leontes
                          You have mistook, my lady,
   Polixenes for Leontes. O thou thing
   Which I'll not call a creature of thy place,
   Lest barbarism, making me the precedent,
85 Should a like language use to all degrees,
   And mannerly distinguishment leave out
   Betwixt the prince and beggar. I have said
   She's an adult'ress; I have said with whom.
   More, she's a traitor, and Camillo is

90 *fedary*: confederate.
91 *know*: acknowledge.
92 *principal*: the person directly responsible.
93 *bed-swerver*: adulteress, one who is false to the marriage-bed.
94 *vulgars*: common people.
   bold'st titles: most crude names.
94-5 *privy . . . escape*: knowledgeable about this recent escape of theirs.

90 A fedary with her, and one that knows
   What she should shame to know herself
   But with her most vile principal—that she's
   A bed-swerver, even as bad as those
   That vulgars give bold'st titles; ay, and privy
95 To this their late escape.
   Hermione
                          No, by my life,
   Privy to none of this. How will this grieve you,
   When you shall come to clearer knowledge, that

98 *thus . . . me*: have called me this in
    public.
    Gentle my lord: my dear lord.
99 *right me*: do me right, make it up to me.
    throughly: fully.

102 *centre*: the whole earth (i.e. the centre of
     the universe—see 'Background', p.144).

104–5 *He who . . . speaks*: any man who
       speaks up for Hermione is himself
       touched with her guilt simply by his
       speaking.
105 *ill planet reigns*: In popular astrology
     certain planets, notably Mars and
     Saturn, were thought to have evil
     influences which were strongest when
     the planets were in the ascendant.
107 *aspect*: position of influence (an
     astrological term).
109 *want*: lack.
     vain: useless.
111 *honourable*: honest.
113–14 *With . . . measure me*: think
        charitably before you judge me.

115 *heard*: listened to, obeyed.

118 *plight*: situation—i.e. her pregnancy.
     good fools: you silly girls. Hermione
     gently chides her waiting-women.
121 *come out*: am indicted.
121–2 *This action . . . grace*: I shall come out
       of this business as a much better
       person. Hermione will regard her
       imprisonment and trial as some kind of
       spiritual testing.
124 *leave*: permission.

You thus have publish'd me! Gentle my lord,
You scarce can right me throughly then to say
100 You did mistake.
    Leontes
               No: if I mistake
In those foundations which I build upon,
The centre is not big enough to bear
A schoolboy's top. Away with her to prison.
He who shall speak for her is afar off guilty
105 But that he speaks.
    Hermione
               There's some ill planet reigns.
I must be patient till the heavens look
With an aspect more favourable. Good my lords,
I am not prone to weeping, as our sex
Commonly are; the want of which vain dew
110 Perchance shall dry your pities: but I have
That honourable grief lodged here which burns
Worse than tears drown. Beseech you all, my lords,
With thoughts so qualified as your charities
Shall best instruct you, measure me; and so
115 The king's will be perform'd!
    Leontes
               Shall I be heard?
    Hermione
Who is't that goes with me? Beseech your highness
My women may be with me, for you see
My plight requires it. Do not weep, good fools:
There is no cause. When you shall know your mistress
120 Has deserv'd prison, then abound in tears
As I come out. This action I now go on
Is for my better grace. Adieu, my lord.
I never wish'd to see you sorry: now
I trust I shall. My women, come, you have leave.
    Leontes
125 Go, do our bidding: hence!
               [*Exeunt* Hermione, *guarded, and* Ladies
    Lord
Beseech your highness, call the queen again.
    Antigonus
Be certain what you do, sir, lest your justice
Prove violence, in the which three great ones suffer:

131 *Please you*: if you want to.
134-6 *I'll keep . . . trust her*: lock up my wife just as I lock my stable-doors (to keep the mares from the stallions); keep her leashed to me as though we were a couple of hounds; and trust her no further than I can see or feel her.
141-2 *You are . . . for't*: you have been deceived, and whoever has put you up to it will be damned for what he has done.
142 *Would*: I wish.
143 *lam-damn*: lambaste; this word (= thrash) seems best to indicate Antigonus's meaning—although his actual word is without precedent—and may be his own coinage.
145 *some five*: about five (years old).
148 *false generations*: bastard children. *co-heirs*: joint-heiresses; the principle of primogeniture did not apply to daughters, who would share the estate between them when there was no male heir.
149 *glib*: castrate.
150 *fair issue*: legitimate children.
151 *smell*: apprehend.
153 *As you . . . thus*: as you can feel when something like *this* is done. Stage business is probably required here—perhaps Leontes strikes something with his hand.
153-4 *and see . . . feel*: and even see what is doing it.

Yourself, your queen, your son.
    Lord
                               For her, my lord,
130 I dare my life lay down, and will do't sir,
Please you t'accept it, that the queen is spotless
I'th'eyes of heaven and to you—I mean
In this which you accuse her.
    Antigonus
                            If it prove
She's otherwise, I'll keep my stables where
135 I lodge my wife; I'll go in couples with her;
Than when I feel and see her no farther trust her:
For every inch of woman in the world,
Ay, every dram of woman's flesh is false,
If she be.
    Leontes
           Hold your peaces.
    Lord
                       Good my lord—
    Antigonus
140 It is for you we speak, not for ourselves.
You are abus'd, and by some putter-on
That will be damn'd for't. Would I knew the villain!
I would lam-damn him. Be she honour-flaw'd,
I have three daughters: the eldest is eleven;
145 The second and the third nine and some five:
If this prove true, they'll pay for't. By mine honour,
I'll geld'em all! Fourteen they shall not see
To bring false generations. They are co-heirs;
And I had rather glib myself than they
150 Should not produce fair issue.
    Leontes
                         Cease, no more!
You smell this business with a sense as cold
As is a dead man's nose; but I do see't and feel't
As you feel doing thus and see withal
The instruments that feel.

154–7 'If Hermione is unfaithful to Leontes
we'll never need to say that honesty is
dead because there will be not the
slightest touch of it in the whole world
to make this rotten earth any better.'
Shakespeare uses 'dungy' only twice—
here and in *Antony and Cleopatra* (*1*, *1*,
35); on both occasions the tone is
contemptuous.

157 *Lack I credit*: don't you believe me.

159 *ground*: subject.

163 *forceful instigation*: powerful instinct.

165–8 *which . . . advice*: if you—whether it's
because you are really insensitive or just
pretending to be stupid—either can't or
won't admit this to yourself (as I have
done), then you can be sure that I don't
want any more of your advice.

170 *Properly ours*: all my own business.

171–2 *You had . . . overture*: you had kept
quiet and worked it out by yourself
without making it public.

175 *familiarity*: intimacy in public.

176 *gross*: shameless.

176–7 *as gross . . . sight*: blatant enough to
give grounds for suspicion without
being seen.

177–8 *naught . . . seeing*: need nothing more
for proof except being seen.

179 *push . . . proceeding*: further this matter.
Camillo's flight has made matters more
urgent, demanding immediate action.

182 *wild*: rash.
   in post: in haste.

183 *sacred Delphos*: the island of Delos,
birthplace of the god Apollo; the name
of the island was often confused with
Delphi, the site of the god's most
famous shrine.

185 *stuff'd sufficiency*: more than adequate
ability.

Antigonus

                 If it be so,
155 We need no grave to bury honesty:
There's not a grain of it the face to sweeten
Of the whole dungy earth.

Leontes

                      What? Lack I credit?

Lord

I had rather you did lack than I, my lord,
Upon this ground; and more it would content me
160 To have her honour true than your suspicion,
Be blam'd for't how you might.

Leontes

                    Why, what need we
Commune with you of this, but rather follow
Our forceful instigation? Our prerogative
Calls not your counsels, but our natural goodness
165 Imparts this; which, if you—or stupefied
Or seeming so in skill—cannot or will not
Relish a truth like us, inform yourselves
We need no more of your advice. The matter,
The loss, the gain, the ord'ring on't, is all
170 Properly ours.

Antigonus

              And I wish, my liege,
You had only in your silent judgement tried it,
Without more overture.

Leontes

                 How could that be?
Either thou art most ignorant by age,
Or thou wert born a fool. Camillo's flight,
175 Added to their familiarity—
Which was as gross as ever touch'd conjecture
That lack'd sight only, naught for approbation
But only seeing, all other circumstances
Made up to th'deed—doth push on this proceeding.
180 Yet, for a greater confirmation—
For in an act of this importance 'twere
Most piteous to be wild—I have dispatch'd in post
To sacred Delphos, to Apollo's temple,
Cleomenes and Dion, whom you know
185 Of stuff'd sufficiency. Now from the oracle

186 *all*: the whole truth.
     had: when I have received it.

191 *he*: i.e. Antigonus.

193 *Come up*: face up.
194 'She should be restrained from getting
     access to me.'
195 *the treachery*: i.e. the plot to murder him
     (mentioned by Leontes in lines 47 and
     89).
198 *raise*: rouse.

They will bring all; whose spiritual counsel, had,
Shall stop or spur me. Have I done well?
Lord
Well done, my lord.
Leontes
Though I am satisfied, and need no more
190 Than what I know, yet shall the oracle
Give rest to th'minds of others, such as he,
Whose ignorant credulity will not
Come up to th'truth. So have we thought it good
From our free person she should be confin'd,
195 Lest that the treachery of the two fled hence
Be left her to perform. Come, follow us:
We are to speak in public; for this business
Will raise us all.
Antigonus
                    [*Aside*] To laughter, as I take it,
If the good truth were known.
                                        [*Exeunt*

Act 2   Scene 2

Hermione is in prison and Paulina, the wife
of Antigonus, visits her—to find that she has
already given birth to her baby. Paulina
volunteers to take the child to Leontes.

1–4 Paulina speaks first to the Gentleman
     (who goes to call the Gaoler), and then
     to herself.

Scene 2

Enter Paulina, *a* Gentleman, *and* Attendants

Paulina
The keeper of the prison, call to him.
Let him have knowledge who I am. [*Exit* Gentleman
                                        Good lady,
No court in Europe is too good for thee:
What dost thou then in prison?

Enter Gentleman *with the* Gaoler

                                    Now, good sir,
5 You know me, do you not?
        Gaoler
                            For a worthy lady,
And one who much I honour.
        Paulina
                                    Pray you then,
Conduct me to the queen.
        Gaoler
                            I may not, madam:

To the contrary I have express commandment.
Paulina
Here's ado
10 To lock up honesty and honour from
Th'access of gentle visitors! Is't lawful, pray you,
To see her women? Any of them? Emilia?
Gaoler
So please you, madam,
To put apart these your attendants, I
15 Shall bring Emilia forth.
Paulina
                                      I pray now, call her.
Withdraw yourselves.
                        [*Exeunt* Gentleman *and* Attendants
Gaoler
                        And, madam,
I must be present at your conference.
Paulina
Well, be't so, prithee.   [*Exit* Gaoler
Here's such ado to make no stain a stain
20 As passes colouring.

Enter Gaoler *with* Emilia

                        Dear gentlewoman,
How fares our gracious lady?
Emilia
As well as one so great and so forlorn
May hold together. On her frights and griefs—
Which never tender lady hath borne greater—
25 She is something before her time deliver'd.
Paulina
A boy?
Emilia
                        A daughter, and a goodly babe,
Lusty, and like to live. The queen receives
Much comfort in't; says, 'My poor prisoner,
I am innocent as you'.
Paulina
                        I dare be sworn.
30 These dangerous, unsafe lunes i'th'king, beshrew
        them!
He must be told on't, and he shall. The office

14 *put apart*: dismiss.

19 'What a carry-on to prove that there's a stain on something which is stainless.'
20 *passes colouring*: beats everything—*both* the dyer's art; *and* all belief; Paulina plays on two senses of 'colour'.

23 *hold together*: bear up.
   On: as a result of.
24 *Which*: than which.
   tender: sensitive.
25 *before her time*: prematurely.

30 *lunes*: fits of lunacy (from *luna* = the moon).

33 *prove honey-mouth'd*: give him any
    flattery.
    blister. Paulina refers to the notion that
    any falsehood would blister the tongue
    of the speaker.
35 *trumpet*: trumpeter (preceding a
    herald—who was often dressed in red to
    deliver an angry message).
39 *to th'loud'st*: at the top of my voice—as
    powerfully as I am able.

44 *free*: voluntary.
    miss: fail to have.

46 *meet*: suitable.

47 *presently*: immediately.

49 *hammer'd of*: was seriously thinking
    about.
50 *durst*: did not dare.
    tempt . . . honour: try asking any official
    who was worthy of the task.

52 *wit*: words of wisdom.

55 *to*: go to.

57 *pass*: let it go out.

Becomes a woman best. I'll take't upon me.
If I prove honey-mouth'd, let my tongue blister,
And never to my red-look'd anger be
35 The trumpet any more. Pray you, Emilia,
Commend my best obedience to the queen.
If she dares trust me with her little babe,
I'll show't the king, and undertake to be
Her advocate to th'loud'st. We do not know
40 How he may soften at the sight o'th'child:
The silence often of pure innocence
Persuades when speaking fails.

    Emilia
                                        Most worthy madam,
Your honour and your goodness is so evident
That your free undertaking cannot miss
45 A thriving issue. There is no lady living
So meet for this great errand. Please your ladyship
To visit the next room, I'll presently
Acquaint the queen of your most noble offer,
Who but today hammer'd of this design,
50 But durst not tempt a minister of honour
Lest she should be denied.

    Paulina
                                    Tell her, Emilia,
I'll use that tongue I have. If wit flow from't
As boldness from my bosom, let't not be doubted
I shall do good.

    Emilia
                    Now be you blest for it!
55 I'll to the queen. Please you come something nearer.

    Gaoler
Madam, if't please the queen to send the babe,
I know not what I shall incur to pass it,
Having no warrant.

    Paulina
                    You need not fear it, sir,
This child was prisoner to the womb, and is
60 By law and process of great nature thence
Freed and enfranchis'd; not a party to
The anger of the king, nor guilty of,
If any be, the trespass of the queen.

Gaoler

I do believe it.

Paulina

65 Do not you fear. Upon mine honour, I
Will stand betwixt you and danger.   [*Exeunt*

Act 2   Scene 3

Alone in his palace, Leontes is meditating on
crime and punishment when he is rudely
interrupted by Paulina. She upbraids him for
his jealous suspicions, and displays his new
daughter for all to see. But he refuses to own
the child, ordering Antigonus to cast it out of
the kingdom. Immediately we hear that the
ambassadors have returned from the oracle.

2 *mere*: nothing but.
3 *in being*: alive.
4 *harlot*: licentious.
5 *arm*: reach, power.
   blank: i.e. the white bull's eye of the
   target in shooting-practice.
6 *level*: aim, range.
   plot-proof: secure against all plotting.
7 *hook to me*: get my hands on.
8 *Given to the fire*: burned alive—the
   penalty for women found guilty of high
   treason and petty treason (which could
   include plotting to murder a husband or
   master).
   moiety: portion.

Scene 3

Enter Leontes

Leontes

Nor night nor day no rest! It is but weakness
To bear the matter thus, mere weakness. If
The cause were not in being—part o'th'cause,
She, th'adult'ress: for the harlot-king
5 Is quite beyond mine arm, out of the blank
And level of my brain, plot-proof; but she
I can hook to me—say that she were gone,
Given to the fire, a moiety of my rest
Might come to me again. Who's there?

Enter Servant

Servant

                                      My lord?

Leontes

10 How does the boy?

Servant

                        He took good rest tonight.
'Tis hop'd his sickness is discharg'd.

Leontes

To see his nobleness!
Conceiving the dishonour of his mother,
He straight declin'd, droop'd, took it deeply,
15 Fasten'd and fix'd the shame on't in himself;

13 *Conceiving*: apprehending the
    significance of.
14 *straight*: instantly.
15 'Became thoroughly ashamed of it
    himself.'

17 *solely*: alone.
18 The Servant is sent to see how *he*
(= Mamillius) is feeling, whilst Leontes'
thoughts switch to *him* (= Polixenes).
19–20 *The very . . . upon me*: any idea of
being revenged on him will blow back
in my face.
21 *his parties*: those on his side.
alliance: allies.

27 *be second to me*: give me your support.

30 *free*: innocent.

35 *each . . . heavings*: every one of his quite
unnecessary sighs.

38 *Honest, as either*: indeed they [her
words] are both 'medicinal' and 'true'.
humour: mood (a recognized medical
and psychological term).

41 *gossips*: godparents (at baptism); the
word had also the modern sense
(= scandalmongers).

Threw off his spirit, his appetite, his sleep,
And downright languish'd. Leave me solely. Go,
See how he fares.   [*Exit* Servant
                Fie, fie, no thought of him!
The very thought of my revenges that way
20 Recoil upon me: in himself too mighty,
And in his parties, his alliance. Let him be
Until a time may serve; for present vengeance
Take it on her. Camillo and Polixenes
Laugh at me, make their pastime at my sorrow.
25 They should not laugh if I could reach them, nor
Shall she within my power.

            Enter Paulina, *carrying a baby, followed by*
            Antigonus, Lords, *and the* Servant, *who*
            try to prevent her

    Lord
                    You must not enter.
    Paulina
Nay, rather, good my lords, be second to me.
Fear you his tyrannous passion more, alas,
Than the queen's life? A gracious, innocent soul,
30 More free than he is jealous.
    Antigonus
                    That's enough.
    Servant
Madam, he hath not slept tonight, commanded
None should come at him.
    Paulina
                    Not so hot, good sir.
I come to bring him sleep. 'Tis such as you,
That creep like shadows by him, and do sigh
35 At each his needless heavings—such as you
Nourish the cause of his awaking. I
Do come with words as med'cinal as true,
Honest, as either, to purge him of that humour
That presses him from sleep.
    Leontes
                    What noise there, ho?
    Paulina
40 No noise, my lord, but needful conference
About some gossips for your highness.

43 *about*: anywhere near.

45 *your displeasure's peril*: at peril of your displeasure.

49 *Commit*: send me to prison.
committing honour: doing what is honourable.
50 *La you now*: there you are.
51 *take the rein*: take control, get the bit between her teeth.
53–7 *who professes . . . seem yours*: The syntax is involved, but the sense is clear enough: most of the courtiers are showing their apparent loyalty to Leontes by encouraging his wicked fantasies (*'comforting your evils'*), but Paulina shows that she is still more loyal in that she dares deny them.

60–1 *would . . . about you*: would challenge you to a duel if I were a man, even the most menial at your court.

62 *makes . . . eyes*: doesn't value his eyes.
63 *hand*: lay a hand on.

Leontes
                                    How?
Away with that audacious lady! Antigonus,
I charg'd thee that she should not come about me.
I knew she would.
          Antigonus
                         I told her so, my lord,
45 On your displeasure's peril, and on mine,
She should not visit you.
          Leontes
                              What? Canst not rule her?
          Paulina
From all dishonesty he can. In this—
Unless he take the course that you have done:
Commit me for committing honour—trust it,
50 He shall not rule me.
          Antigonus
                         La you now, you hear.
When she will take the rein, I let her run;
But she'll not stumble.
          Paulina
                         Good my liege, I come—
And I beseech you hear me, who professes
Myself your loyal servant, your physician,
55 Your most obedient counsellor; yet that dares
Less appear so in comforting your evils
Than such as most seem yours—I say, I come
From your good queen.
          Leontes
                              Good queen?
          Paulina
Good queen, my lord, good queen, I say good
          queen;
60 And would by combat make her good, so were I
A man, the worst about you.
          Leontes
                              Force her hence.
          Paulina
Let him that makes but trifles of his eyes
First hand me. On mine own accord I'll off,
But first I'll do my errand. The good queen—

65 For she is good—hath brought you forth a daughter:
Here 'tis; commends it to your blessing.

She lays down the child

Leontes
                                                    Out!
A mankind witch! Hence with her, out o'door!
A most intelligencing bawd!
Paulina
                                        Not so:
I am as ignorant in that as you
70 In so entitling me; and no less honest
Than you are mad; which is enough, I'll warrant,
As this world goes, to pass for honest.
Leontes
                                            Traitors!
Will you not push her out? Give her the bastard.
[*To* Antigonus] Thou dotard, thou art woman-tir'd,
    unroosted
75 By thy Dame Partlet here. Take up the bastard!
Take't up, I say! Give't to thy crone.
Paulina
                                        For ever
Unvenerable be thy hands if thou
Tak'st up the princess by that forced baseness
Which he has put upon't!
Leontes
                                        He dreads his wife.
Paulina
80 So I would you did: then 'twere past all doubt
You'd call your children yours.
Leontes
                                        A nest of traitors!
Antigonus
I am none, by this good light!
Paulina
                                        Nor I, nor any
But one that's here, and that's himself: for he
The sacred honour of himself, his queen's,
85 His hopeful son's, his babe's, betrays to slander,
Whose sting is sharper than the sword's; and will
    not—

67 *mankind*: virago-like, unfeminine.
68 *intelligencing*: secretive.
bawd: go-between, one who passes messages between clandestine lovers.
69 *ignorant*: unskilled.
70 *entitling me*: giving me that name.
74 *dotard*: old fool.
woman-tir'd: hen-pecked; 'to tire' is a term used in falconry (= to pull, tear).
75 *Partlet*: Chanticleer and Partlet are the traditional names of the cock and the hen.
76 *crone*: old woman.
78–9 *by that . . . upon't*: accepting that false description of 'bastard' which he has unjustly given it.
80 *would*: wish.
85 *hopeful son*: son and heir.
86–9 *will not . . . opinion*: will never uproot his suspicion—and because he's the king, worse luck, no one can force him to.

For, as the case now stands, it is a curse
He cannot be compell'd to't—once remove
The root of his opinion, which is rotten
90 As ever oak or stone was sound.

Leontes

                                        A callat

90 *callat*: scold, nag.

91 *late*: recently.

92 *bait*: torment. Leontes makes a pun with 'beat'.

Of boundless tongue, who late hath beat her husband,
And now baits me! This brat is none of mine:
It is the issue of Polixenes.
Hence with it, and together with the dam
95 Commit them to the fire!

Paulina

                                        It is yours;

96 *lay . . . charge*: accuse you with an old proverb.

97 *So . . . worse*: it's all the worse for resembling you.

98–9 *print . . . matter . . . copy*: The baby is a miniature reprint of the father.

100 *trick of's frown*: the way he (i.e. Leontes) wrinkles his face.
valley: little groove or indentation.

And, might we lay th'old proverb to your charge,
So like you, 'tis the worse. Behold, my lords,
Although the print be little, the whole matter
And copy of the father: eye, nose, lip;
100 The trick of's frown; his forehead; nay, the valley,
The pretty dimples of his chin and cheek; his smiles;
The very mould and frame of hand, nail, finger.
And thou, good goddess Nature, which hast made it
So like to him that got it, if thou hast

104 *got*: begot.

106 *yellow*: i.e. the colour of jealousy.

106–7 *suspect . . . husband's*: question her husband's fidelity (or even her own). Paulina's passion leads to comic excess.

108 *losel*: scoundrel.

109 *stay*: stop.

105 The ordering of the mind too, 'mongst all colours
No yellow in't, lest she suspect, as he does,
Her children not her husband's.

Leontes

                                        A gross hag!

And, losel, thou art worthy to be hang'd,
That wilt not stay her tongue.

Antigonus

                                        Hang all the husbands

109–11 This observation is perhaps spoken by Antigonus 'aside' from Leontes—but out directly to the audience.

110 That cannot do that feat, you'll leave yourself
Hardly one subject.

Leontes

                                        Once more, take her hence.

Paulina

A most unworthy and unnatural lord
Can do no more.

Leontes

                                        I'll ha'thee burn'd.

Paulina

                                        I care not:

114–15 *It is . . . burns in't*: being burned alive (the extreme punishment for heresy) is not enough in itself to prove that the victim is a heretic; *or perhaps*, the one lighting the fire—i.e. Leontes—is the heretic, not the woman whom he condemns to burn in it.

118 *weak-hing'd*: disconnected, illogical. *something savours*: smells a bit.

121–2 *Were I . . . life*: would she be still alive if I were really a tyrant.

122–3 *She . . . me one*: she wouldn't dare to call me a tyrant if she thought I really was one.

125 *to*: after. *Jove*: Jupiter.
126 *What . . . hands*: you don't need to lay hands on me.
127 *so tender . . . follies*: encouraging him like this in his crazy ideas.

131 *Even thou*: yes, you.

139 *bastard*: bastard's—i.e. the baby's. *proper*: own.

It is an heretic that makes the fire,
115 Not she which burns in't. I'll not call you tyrant;
But this most cruel usage of your queen—
Not able to produce more accusation
Than your own weak-hing'd fancy—something savours
Of tyranny, and will ignoble make you,
120 Yea, scandalous to the world.

Leontes

On your allegiance,
Out of the chamber with her! Were I a tyrant,
Where were her life? She durst not call me so,
If she did know me one. Away with her!

They slowly push her towards the door

Paulina
I pray you, do not push me, I'll be gone.
125 Look to your babe, my lord; 'tis yours. Jove send her
A better guiding spirit! What needs these hands?
You that are thus so tender o'er his follies
Will never do him good, not one of you.
So, so. Farewell, we are gone.

[*Exit*

Leontes
130 Thou, traitor, hast set on thy wife to this.
My child? Away with't! Even thou, that hast
A heart so tender o'er it, take it hence
And see it instantly consum'd with fire:
Even thou, and none but thou. Take it up straight!
135 Within this hour bring me word 'tis done,
And by good testimony, or I'll seize thy life,
With what thou else call'st thine. If thou refuse,
And wilt encounter with my wrath, say so:
The bastard brains with these my proper hands
140 Shall I dash out. Go, take it to the fire,
For thou set'st on thy wife.

Antigonus

I did not, sir.
These lords, my noble fellows, if they please,
Can clear me in't.

Lords

We can. My royal liege,

He is not guilty of her coming hither.
  Leontes
145 You're liars all.
  Lord
  Beseech your highness, give us better credit.
  We have always truly serv'd you, and beseech'
  So to esteem of us; and on our knees we beg,
  As recompense of our dear services
150 Past and to come, that you do change this purpose,
  Which being so horrible, so bloody, must
  Lead on to some foul issue. We all kneel.
  Leontes
  I am a feather for each wind that blows.
  Shall I live on to see this bastard kneel
155 And call me father? Better burn it now
  Than curse it then. But be it: let it live.
  It shall not neither [*To* Antigonus] You, sir, come
    you hither:
  You that have been so tenderly officious
  With Lady Margery, your midwife there,
160 To save this bastard's life—for 'tis a bastard,
  So sure as this beard's grey—what will you adventure
  To save this brat's life?
  Antigonus
                    Anything, my lord,
  That my ability may undergo,
  And nobleness impose—at least thus much:
165 I'll pawn the little blood which I have left
  To save the innocent—anything possible.
  Leontes
  It shall be possible. Swear by this sword
  Thou wilt perform my bidding.
  Antigonus
  [*His hand upon the hilt*]   I will, my lord.
  Leontes
  Mark and perform it, see'st thou? For the fail
170 Of any point in't shall not only be
  Death to thyself, but to thy lewd-tongued wife,
  Whom for this time we pardon. We enjoin thee,
  As thou art liegeman to us, that thou carry
  This female bastard hence, and that thou bear it
175 To some remote and desert place, quite out

147 *beseech'*: beseech you.

159 *Lady Margery*: that old hen—a term of
   abuse like 'Dame Partlet' (line 75).
   midwife: This too is contemptuous.
161 *this beard*: i.e. Antigonus's beard, which
   he perhaps pulls or points at; Leontes
   (see *1, 2, 154 note*) can hardly be
   referring to his own beard.
   adventure: venture, risk.

165 *the little blood*: i.e. the few years of life.

167 *by this sword*: The cross-piece of the
   sword was appropriate for the swearing
   of oaths *in a Christian culture*.

169 *fail*: failure.
173 *liegeman*: A feudal term for one owing
   total allegiance to his lord.

178 *favour of the climate*: chances of the
     weather.
     strange: Leontes makes play with two
     senses of the word (= *both* unusual, *and
     also* foreign, from overseas). Leontes
     argues that the child came in an
     unusual manner because a foreigner
     (i.e. Polixenes) was responsible for it.
179 *in justice*: in all fairness.
180 'At the risk of being physically tortured
     and eternally damned (for breaking
     your religious oath).'
181 *commend*: commit.
     strangely to some place: to some foreign
     place, *or*, as a foreigner somewhere.
182 *chance*: fortune, luck.
183 *present*: instant, immediate.
188 *Like offices*: similar works: legend has it
     that Romulus and Remus, the founders
     of Rome, were reared by a she-wolf.
189 *In . . . require*: more than you deserve
     for doing this deed.
     blessing: may heaven send mercy;
     Antigonus now addresses the baby.
191 *loss*: destruction.

192 *posts*: messengers.

196 *Hasting*: hastening.

197 *beyond accompt*: unprecedented, beyond
     expectation.

199 *suddenly*: without delay, immediately.

201 *session*: court of law.

204 *While*: as long as.

Of our dominions; and that there thou leave it,
Without more mercy, to its own protection
And favour of the climate. As by strange fortune
It came to us, I do in justice charge thee,
180 On thy soul's peril and thy body's torture,
That thou commend it strangely to some place
Where chance may nurse or end it. Take it up.

Antigonus
I swear to do this, though a present death
Had been more merciful. Come on, poor babe,
185 Some powerful spirit instruct the kites and ravens
To be thy nurses! Wolves and bears, they say,
Casting their savageness aside, have done
Like offices of pity. Sir, be prosperous
In more than this deed does require! And blessing
190 Against this cruelty fight on thy side,
Poor thing, condemn'd to loss!

[*Exit with the child*

Leontes
                              No, I'll not rear
Another's issue.

Enter a Servant

Servant
                 Please your highness, posts
From those you sent to th'oracle are come
An hour since: Cleomenes and Dion,
195 Being well arriv'd from Delphos, are both landed,
Hasting to th'court.

Lord
                    So please you, sir, their speed
Hath been beyond accompt.

Leontes
                          Twenty-three days
They have been absent. 'Tis good speed; foretells
The great Apollo suddenly will have
200 The truth of this appear. Prepare you, lords.
Summon a session, that we may arraign
Our most disloyal lady: for as she hath
Been publicly accus'd, so shall she have
A just and open trial. While she lives
205 My heart will be a burden to me. Leave me,
And think upon my bidding.

[*Exeunt*

Act 3

Act 3   Scene 1

Cleomenes and Dion, the two ambassadors, have been breathing a very different air from that of Leontes' court. They are now returned to share their experience, and to deliver the oracle's verdict.

1   *delicate*: delightful.
2   *the isle*: i.e. Delos, the birthplace (sometimes known as Delphos) of the god Apollo.
4   *most . . . me*: that's what most impressed me.
    habits: vestments.

10 *Kin . . . thunder*: Appearances and utterances of the gods are often associated with thunder—which itself is the instrument of Jupiter, king of the Roman deities.
11 *event*: outcome.

14 *The time . . . on't*: the time has been well spent.

16 *forcing*: unfairly thrusting.

17 *carriage*: conduct, management.

19 *divine*: priest.

Scene 1

Enter Cleomenes *and* Dion

Cleomenes
The climate's delicate, the air most sweet,
Fertile the isle, the temple much surpassing
The common praise it bears.
            Dion
                            I shall report,
For most it caught me, the celestial habits—
5 Methinks I so should term them—and the reverence
Of the grave wearers. O, the sacrifice!
How ceremonious, solemn, and unearthly
It was i'th'off'ring!
            Cleomenes
                        But of all, the burst
And the ear-deaf'ning voice o'th'oracle,
10 Kin to Jove's thunder, so surpris'd my sense
That I was nothing.
            Dion
                        If th'event o'th'journey
Prove as successful to the queen—O, be't so!—
As it hath been to us rare, pleasant, speedy,
The time is worth the use on't.
            Cleomenes
                                Great Apollo
15 Turn all to th'best! These proclamations,
So forcing faults upon Hermione,
I little like.
            Dion
                The violent carriage of it
Will clear or end the business. When the oracle,
Thus by Apollo's great divine seal'd up,

20 *contents*: true facts.
    discover: reveal.
21 *fresh horses*: The ambassadors have
    clearly travelled some distance inland
    after reaching the coast of Sicilia.

20 Shall the contents discover, something rare
    Even then will rush to knowledge. Go: fresh horses!
    And gracious be the issue.

                                        [*Exeunt*

Scene 2

Act 3   Scene 2

The court assembles for the trial. With
dignity and courage Hermione defends
herself, and at length she appeals to the
judgement of the oracle. But when this is
delivered, and her innocence proclaimed,
Leontes refuses to accept the verdict of the
god. Hermione collapses—and news is
brought of the sudden decline and death of
the young Mamillius. Overcome by remorse,
Leontes withdraws his allegations, but it is
too late! Paulina informs him that his wife is
dead.

Enter Leontes, Lords, *and* Officers

   Leontes
This sessions, to our great grief we pronounce,
Even pushes 'gainst our heart: the party tried
The daughter of a king, our wife, and one
Of us too much belov'd. Let us be clear'd
5 Of being tyrannous, since we so openly
Proceed in justice, which shall have due course,
Even to the guilt or the purgation.
Produce the prisoner.

1 *sessions*: trial.
  we: I (Leontes uses the 'royal plural').
2 *Even . . . heart*: strikes right to my heart.
  tried: to be tried.
5 *openly*: publicly.
6 *have due course*: be carried out in the proper manner.
7 *guilt*: declaration of guilt.
  purgation: acquittal.

17 *pretence*: purpose, plot.

24 *boot me*: do me any good.

26 *counted*: accounted.
  express it: speak the words.
27 *so*: i.e. as falsehood.

35 *history*: stories, plays.
  pattern: give precedent for.
36 *take*: fascinate.
37 *fellow*: partner.
  owe: own.
38 *moiety*: share.
39 *hopeful*: promising, aspiring.
40 *prate*: plead in vain.
  'fore: in front of.
41 *Who please*: whoever pleases.
41–2 *For life . . . spare*: as for my life, I value it as much as I value grief, which is something I would rather be without.
42–4 *for honour . . . stand for*: but honour is a heritage that descends from me to my children, and it is only this that I am fighting for.

Officer
It is his highness' pleasure that the queen
10 Appear in person here in court.

Enter Hermione, *guarded*, Paulina, *and*
Ladies *attending*

Silence!

Leontes
Read the indictment.

Officer
[*Reads*] *Hermione, queen to the worthy Leontes, king of*
Sicilia, thou art here accused and arraigned of high
treason, in committing adultery with Polixenes,
15 *king of Bohemia, and conspiring with Camillo to take*
away the life of our sovereign lord the king, thy royal
husband; the pretence whereof being by circumstances
partly laid open, thou, Hermione, contrary to the faith
and allegiance of a true subject, didst counsel and aid
20 *them, for their better safety, to fly away by night.*

Hermione
Since what I am to say must be but that
Which contradicts my accusation, and
The testimony on my part no other
But what comes from myself, it shall scarce boot me
25 To say 'Not guilty': mine integrity
Being counted falsehood, shall, as I express it,
Be so receiv'd. But thus: if powers divine
Behold our human actions—as they do—
I doubt not then but innocence shall make
30 False accusation blush, and tyranny
Tremble at patience. You, my lord, best know—
Who least will seem to do so—my past life
Hath been as continent, as chaste, as true,
As I am now unhappy; which is more
35 Than history can pattern, though devis'd
And play'd to take spectators. For behold me,
A fellow of the royal bed, which owe
A moiety of the throne, a great king's daughter,
The mother to a hopeful prince, here standing
40 To prate and talk for life and honour 'fore
Who please to come and hear. For life, I prize it
As I weigh grief, which I would spare; for honour,
'Tis a derivative from me to mine,

And only that I stand for. I appeal
45 To your own conscience, sir, before Polixenes
Came to your court, how I was in your grace,
How merited to be so; since he came,
With what encounter so uncurrent I
Have strain'd t'appear thus: if one jot beyond
50 The bound of honour, or in act or will
That way inclining, harden'd be the hearts
Of all that hear me, and my near'st of kin
Cry fie upon my grave!

Leontes
                    I ne'er heard yet
That any of these bolder vices wanted
55 Less impudence to gainsay what they did
Than to perform it first.

Hermione
                    That's true enough,
Though 'tis a saying, sir, not due to me.

Leontes
You will not own it.

Hermione
                    More than mistress of
Which comes to me in name of fault I must not
60 At all acknowledge. For Polixenes,
With whom I am accus'd, I do confess
I lov'd him as in honour he requir'd:
With such a kind of love as might become
A lady like me; with a love even such,
65 So and no other, as yourself commanded;
Which not to have done I think had been in me
Both disobedience and ingratitude
To you and toward your friend, whose love had spoke
Even since it could speak, from an infant, freely
70 That it was yours. Now, for conspiracy,
I know not how it tastes, though it be dish'd
For me to try how. All I know of it
Is that Camillo was an honest man;
And why he left your court the gods themselves,
75 Wotting no more than I, are ignorant.

Leontes
You knew of his departure, as you know
What you have underta'en to do in's absence.

44–9 *I appeal . . . thus*: Hermione first begs Leontes to remember how she used to deserve his love *before* Polixenes visited the court, and then to explain what it is that she has done to merit his present arraignment of her.

46 *grace*: favour.

48 *encounter*: behaviour, conduct.
uncurrent: extraordinary, debased (the image is from coinage).

50 *or . . . will*: either in fact or in intention.

55 *gainsay*: deny.

57 *due*: applicable.

58–60 *More than . . . acknowledge*: I will not confess to anything more than what is now being called a 'fault'. Hermione admits her friendship with Polixenes whilst denying the 'bolder vices' (line 54) with which she has been charged.

62 *requir'd*: deserved.

63 *become*: be appropriate for.

70 *for*: as for.

71–2 *I know . . . how*: I do not know anything about it, and I would not recognize it if it were given to me on a plate.

75 *Wotting*: if they know.

77 *What . . . to do*: i.e. to murder Leontes.

80   *in the level*: within the range (as of a gun).
     dreams: fantasies, delusions.
84   *of your fact*: guilty of your crime.
85   'Denying this is more trouble than it's worth.'
85–90 *for as . . . death*: just as your child has been treated like the outcast it is, with no father acknowledging it—and you are more guilty than the child in this—so you can't expect anything less than a death sentence for yourself from my judgement.
91   *bug*: bugbear, bogy.
     would: want to.
92   *commodity*: advantage, enjoyment.
94   *give*: account.
98   *Starr'd most unluckily*: born under a very unlucky star.
100 *Hal'd*: dragged.
     on every post: posted up everywhere on public notices.
101 *immodest*: excessive.
102 *childbed privilege*: the right to stay in bed for a period after giving birth.
     'longs: belongs.
103 *of all fashions*: of every rank, regardless of class.
104 *i'th'open air*: Fresh air was considered a health-hazard for invalids.

105 *got . . . limit*: been given time to recover my strength.
108–9 *no life . . . free*: I do not ask for life, which means nothing to me, but I want to clear my honour.
111 *all . . . else*: since there's no other evidence.
113 *rigour and not law*: tyranny and not justice; the phrase comes from *Pandosto*.
     Your honours: Hermione addresses the court.

Hermione

Sir,
You speak a language that I understand not.
80 My life stands in the level of your dreams,
Which I'll lay down.
       Leontes
                      Your actions are my dreams.
You had a bastard by Polixenes,
And I but dream'd it. As you were past all shame—
Those of your fact are so—so past all truth;
85 Which to deny concerns more than avails: for as
Thy brat hath been cast out, like to itself,
No father owning it—which is indeed
More criminal in thee than it—so thou
Shalt feel our justice, in whose easiest passage
90 Look for no less than death.
       Hermione
                      Sir, spare your threats!
The bug which you would fright me with I seek.
To me can life be no commodity:
The crown and comfort of my life, your favour,
I do give lost, for I do feel it gone,
95 But know not how it went. My second joy,
And first-fruits of my body, from his presence
I am barr'd, like one infectious. My third comfort,
Starr'd most unluckily, is from my breast—
The innocent milk in its most innocent mouth—
100 Hal'd out to murder. Myself on every post
Proclaim'd a strumpet; with immodest hatred
The childbed privilege denied, which 'longs
To women of all fashion; lastly, hurried
Here to this place, i'th'open air, before
105 I have got strength of limit. Now, my liege,
Tell me what blessings I have here alive
That I should fear to die. Therefore proceed.
But yet hear this—mistake me not: no life,
I prize it not a straw; but for mine honour,
110 Which I would free—if I shall be condemn'd
Upon surmises, all proofs sleeping else
But what your jealousies awake, I tell you
'Tis rigour and not law. Your honours all,
I do refer me to the oracle:
115 Apollo be my judge!

Lord

This your request
Is altogether just. Therefore bring forth,
And in Apollo's name, his oracle.

[*Exeunt certain* Officers

Hermione

The Emperor of Russia was my father.
O that he were alive, and here beholding
120 His daughter's trial! That he did but see
The flatness of my misery; yet with eyes
Of pity, not revenge!

Enter Officers, *with* Cleomenes *and* Dion

Officer

You here shall swear upon this sword of justice
That you, Cleomenes and Dion, have
125 Been both at Delphos, and from thence have brought
This seal'd-up oracle, by the hand deliver'd
Of great Apollo's priest; and that since then
You have not dared to break the holy seal,
Nor read the secrets in't.

Cleomenes and **Dion**

All this we swear.

Leontes

130 Break up the seals and read.

Officer

[*Reads*] *Hermione is chaste; Polixenes blameless; Camillo
a true subject; Leontes a jealous tyrant; his innocent babe
truly begotten; and the king shall live without an heir, if
that which is lost be not found.*

Lords

135 Now blessed be the great Apollo!

Hermione

Praised!

Leontes

Hast thou read truth?

Officer

Ay, my lord, even so
As it is here set down.

Leontes

There is no truth at all i'th'oracle!
The sessions shall proceed: this is mere falsehood.

121 *flatness of my misery*: my absolute and
unrelieved misery.

Enter Servant

Servant
140 My lord the king, the king!
Leontes

What is the business?
Servant
O sir, I shall be hated to report it:
The prince your son, with mere conceit and fear
Of the queen's speed, is gone.
Leontes

How! Gone?
Servant

Is dead.
Leontes
Apollo's angry, and the heavens themselves
145 Do strike at my injustice.

Hermione *faints*

How now there!
Paulina
This news is mortal to the queen: look down
And see what death is doing.
Leontes

Take her hence.
Her heart is but o'ercharg'd; she will recover.
I have too much believ'd mine own suspicion.
150 Beseech you, tenderly apply to her
Some remedies for life.
[*Exeunt* Paulina *and* Ladies, *bearing* Hermione
Apollo, pardon
My great profaneness 'gainst thine oracle!
I'll reconcile me to Polixenes;
New woo my queen; recall the good Camillo—
155 Whom I proclaim a man of truth, of mercy:
For, being transported by my jealousies
To bloody thoughts and to revenge, I chose
Camillo for the minister to poison
My friend Polixenes; which had been done,
160 But that the good mind of Camillo tardied
My swift command, though I with death and with
Reward did threaten and encourage him,
Not doing it and being done. He, most humane,

141 *to report*: for reporting.
142–3 *with mere . . . speed*: just by thinking about what might happen to the queen.

148 *o'ercharged*: over-wrought, stressed.

156 *transported*: carried away.
157 *bloody*: bloodthirsty.

159 *had*: would have.
160 *tardied*: put off, delayed.
163 *Not doing . . . done*: Camillo was threatened with death if he did not murder Polixenes, and promised a reward when the murder was done.

165 *Unclasp'd*: opened up, revealed.
     practice: plot.
166-7 *to the . . . commended*: resigned himself
     to taking all the risks of gambling with
     the unknown.
168 *No . . . honour*: with his honour as his
     only possession.
     glisters: glistens, glitters.
169 *piety*: devotion, dedication to truth.
170 *Woe the while*: alas for the present time.

171 *cut my lace*: i.e. the tight laces of her
     bodice or corsets; Paulina feels faint.

173 *studied*: well thought-out.
174 *flaying*: skinning alive.
175 *In leads or oils*: in cauldrons of boiling
     lead or boiling oil.

179 *green and idle*: feeble and futile.
180 *they*: i.e. his jealousies and tyranny.
182 *bygone*: previous, earlier.
     but spices: only samples, foretastes.
184 *of a fool*: for a fool, as regards being a
     fool.
186-7 *poison'd . . . kill a king*: Unless Camillo
     had confided in her before he left the
     court, Paulina could not have known
     about this, but Shakespeare seems to
     have forgotten—and it is unlikely that a
     theatre audience would notice the slip.
187-8 *poor . . . standing by*: these were petty
     crimes in comparison with the other
     monstrosities.
190 *or none or little*: the least of these.
191 *shed . . . fire*: wept in hell.
     ere done't: rather than have done it.
192 *is't . . . thee*: are you directly accused of.
194 *high*: exalted, noble.
     tender: young.
195 *conceive*: believe.
196 *Blemish'd*: cast a stain on.
     dam: mother.
197 *Laid . . . answer*: made an accusation
     against you.
198 *said*: spoken.

And fill'd with honour, to my kingly guest
165 Unclasp'd my practice, quit his fortunes here—
Which you knew great—and to the hazard
Of all incertainties himself commended,
No richer than his honour. How he glisters
Through my rust! And how his piety
170 Does my deeds make the blacker!

          Enter Paulina

Paulina
                              Woe the while!
O cut my lace, lest my heart, cracking it,
Break too!
     Lord
          What fit is this, good lady?
     Paulina
What studied torments, tyrant, hast for me?
What wheels? Racks? Fires? What flaying? Boiling
175 In leads or oils? What old or newer torture
Must I receive, whose every word deserves
To taste of thy most worst? Thy tyranny,
Together working with thy jealousies—
Fancies too weak for boys, too green and idle
180 For girls of nine—O think what they have done,
And then run mad indeed, stark mad! For all
Thy bygone fooleries were but spices of it.
That thou betray'dst Polixenes 'twas nothing:
That did but show thee of a fool inconstant,
185 And damnable ingrateful. Nor was't much
Thou wouldst have poison'd good Camillo's honour
To have him kill a king—poor trespasses,
More monstrous standing by: whereof I reckon
The casting forth to crows thy baby daughter
190 To be or none or little, though a devil
Would have shed water out of fire ere done't;
Nor is't directly laid to thee, the death
Of the young prince, whose honourable thoughts—
Thoughts high for one so tender—cleft the heart
195 That could conceive a gross and foolish sire
Blemish'd his gracious dam. This is not, no,
Laid to thy answer. But the last—O lords,
When I have said, cry woe! The queen, the queen,

200 *dropp'd down*: i.e. from heaven.

203 *Tincture . . . eye*: colour to her lips or lustre to her eyes.

207 *woes can stir*: lamentations can expiate.

210 *still*: always, continually.

215 *have made fault*: are at fault; the lord speaks to Paulina.

220-1 *What's gone . . . grief*: a proverbial saying—'no use crying over spilt milk'.

223 *minded you*: put you in mind.

226 *lo, fool again*: there I go being stupid again; Paulina constantly and deliberately reminds Leontes of his mistakes.

229 *take . . . to you*: be patient in your suffering.

230-1 *speak . . . the truth*: you were only saying what was absolutely true.

The sweet'st, dear'st creature's dead! And vengeance for't
200 Not dropp'd down yet.
   Lords
        The higher powers forbid!
   Paulina
I say she's dead; I'll swear't. If word nor oath
Prevail not, go and see. If you can bring
Tincture or lustre in her lip, her eye,
Heat outwardly or breath within, I'll serve you
205 As I would do the gods. But, O thou tyrant,
Do not repent these things, for they are heavier
Than all thy woes can stir. Therefore betake thee
To nothing but despair. A thousand knees,
Ten thousand years together, naked, fasting,
210 Upon a barren mountain, and still winter
In storm perpetual, could not move the gods
To look that way thou wert.
   Leontes
        Go on, go on:
Thou canst not speak too much; I have deserv'd
All tongues to talk their bitt'rest.
   Lord
          Say no more.
215 Howe'er the business goes, you have made fault
I'th'boldness of your speech.
   Paulina
        I am sorry for't.
All faults I make, when I shall come to know them,
I do repent. Alas, I have show'd too much
The rashness of a woman! He is touch'd
220 To th'noble heart. What's gone and what's past help
Should be past grief. Do not receive affliction
At my petition, I beseech you; rather
Let me be punish'd, that have minded you
Of what you should forget. Now, good my liege,
225 Sir, royal sir, forgive a foolish woman.
The love I bore your queen—lo, fool again!
I'll speak of her no more, nor of your children;
I'll not remember you of my own lord,
Who is lost too. Take your patience to you,
230 And I'll say nothing.

Leontes

Thou didst speak but well
When most the truth; which I receive much better
Than to be pitied of thee. Prithee, bring me
To the dead bodies of my queen and son.
One grave shall be for both: upon them shall
235 The causes of their death appear, unto
Our shame perpetual. Once a day I'll visit
The chapel where they lie, and tears shed there
Shall be my recreation. So long as nature
Will bear up with this exercise, so long
240 I daily vow to use it. Come,
And lead me to these sorrows.   [*Exeunt*

234 *them*: i.e. the monuments of the grave.

238 *recreation*: The word contains the senses
of *both* 'refreshment' *and* 're-creation'.

239–40 *nature . . . exercise*: I have the
strength to follow this practice; *exercise*
has also the sense of 'religious
observance'.

Act 3   Scene 3

Landing on the deserted shore of a foreign country, Antigonus abandons the baby to its fate—and meets his own! A Shepherd finds the child.

1 *perfect*: absolutely certain.
2 *deserts*: lonely places.

4 *present*: imminent.
5 *have in hand*: are doing now.

8 *Look to thy bark*: look after your boat.

10 *loud*: rough.

Scene 3

Enter Antigonus *with the child, and a* Mariner

Antigonus
Thou art perfect, then, our ship hath touch'd upon
The deserts of Bohemia?

Mariner
                              Ay, my lord, and fear
We have landed in ill time: the skies look grimly,
And threaten present blusters. In my conscience,
5 The heavens with that we have in hand are angry
And frown upon's.

Antigonus
Their sacred wills be done! Go, get aboard;
Look to thy bark. I'll not be long before
I call upon thee.

Mariner
                              Make your best haste, and go not
10 Too far i'th'land: 'tis like to be loud weather.

Besides, this place is famous for the creatures
Of prey that keep upon't.
> **Antigonus**
> > Go thou away:
I'll follow instantly.
> **Mariner**
> > I am glad at heart
To be so rid o'th'business.   [*Exit*
> **Antigonus**
> > Come, poor babe.

15 *dead*: Antigonus can have no knowledge
of the events in Leontes' court, but the
appearance of Hermione in his dream
was enough to convince him that she
has been put to death.
19 *some another*: sometimes on the other.
20–1 *a vessel . . . becoming*: Antigonus
images Hermione as a beautiful ship
under full sail.
22 *very sanctity*: the embodiment of
saintliness, a real saint.
24 *gasping*: struggling for breath.
25 *the fury spent*: when the emotional
outburst was over.
anon: at once.

15 I have heard, but not believ'd, the spirits o'th'dead
May walk again: if such thing be, thy mother
Appear'd to me last night; for ne'er was dream
So like a waking. To me comes a creature,
Sometimes her head on one side, some another:
20 I never saw a vessel of like sorrow,
So fill'd and so becoming. In pure white robes,
Like very sanctity, she did approach
My cabin where I lay; thrice bow'd before me,
And, gasping to begin some speech, her eyes
25 Became two spouts; the fury spent, anon
Did this break from her: 'Good Antigonus,
Since fate, against thy better disposition,
Hath made thy person for the thrower-out
Of my poor babe, according to thy oath,
30 Places remote enough are in Bohemia:
There weep, and leave it crying; and for the babe
Is counted lost for ever, Perdita
I prithee call't. For this ungentle business,
Put on thee by my lord, thou ne'er shalt see
35 Thy wife Paulina more.' And so, with shrieks,
She melted into air. Affrighted much,
I did in time collect myself, and thought
This was so, and no slumber. Dreams are toys:
Yet for this once, yea superstitiously,
40 I will be squar'd by this. I do believe
Hermione hath suffer'd death, and that
Apollo would, this being indeed the issue
Of King Polixenes, it should here be laid,
Either for life or death, upon the earth

32 *Perdita*: The name means 'the lost one'.

34 *Put*: imposed.
35 *shrieks*: These were thought to be the
typical cries of a ghost.
36 *Affrighted much*: very frightened indeed.

38 *toys*: trivial matters, things of no
substance.
39 *superstitiously*: punctiliously: but the
modern meaning may be also present,
producing a kind of pun.
40 *squar'd*: ruled, directed.
42 *would*: desires, wishes.

45 *speed*: fare.

45 Of its right father. Blossom, speed thee well!

He lays down the child, and a scroll

46 *character*: written account of your life.
these: i.e. the jewels and 'fairy gold' that
the Shepherd will find at line 119.

There lie, and there thy character;

He lays down a box

47–8 *breed thee . . . thine*: pay for your
upbringing, my pretty one, and still
have something left over that you can
call your own.

50 *loss*: destruction, being cast away.
Weep I cannot: Antigonus cannot obey
Hermione's injunction of line 31.

52 *by oath*: i.e. his oath to Leontes.

53 *like*: likely.

55 *savage clamour*: Antigonus hears the
roaring of the bear.

56 *This is the chase*: the hunt is on.

there these,
Which may, if fortune please, both breed thee, pretty,
And still rest thine. The storm begins. Poor wretch,
That for thy mother's fault art thus expos'd

50 To loss and what may follow! Weep I cannot,
But my heart bleeds; and most accurs'd am I
To be by oath enjoin'd to this. Farewell!
The day frowns more and more. Thou'rt like to have
A lullaby too rough: I never saw

55 The heavens so dim by day.—A savage clamour!
Well may I get aboard! This is the chase.
I am gone for ever!   [*Exit, pursued by a bear*

Enter an old Shepherd

Shepherd

I would there were no age between ten and three-
and-twenty, or that youth would sleep out the rest:
60 for there is nothing in the between but getting
wenches with child, wronging the ancientry, stealing,
fighting. Hark you now: would any but these boiled
brains of nineteen and two-and-twenty hunt this
weather? They have scared away two of my best
65 sheep, which I fear the wolf will sooner find than the
master. If anywhere I have them, 'tis by the seaside,
browsing of ivy. Good luck, an't be thy will!

He sees the child

What have we here? Mercy on's, a barne! A very
pretty barne. A boy or a child, I wonder? A pretty
70 one, a very pretty one. Sure, some scape. Though I
am not bookish, yet I can read waiting gentlewoman
in the scape: this has been some stair-work, some
trunk-work, some behind-door-work. They were
warmer that got this than the poor thing is here. I'll
75 take it up for pity—yet I'll tarry till my son come: he
hallowed but even now. Whoa-ho-hoa!

Enter Clown

Clown

Hilloa, loa!

Shepherd

What! Art so near? If thou'lt see a thing to talk on
when thou art dead and rotten, come hither. What
80 ail'st thou, man?

Clown

I have seen two such sights, by sea and by land! But
I am not to say it is a sea, for it is now the sky:
betwixt the firmament and it you cannot thrust a
bodkin's point.

Shepherd

85 Why, boy, how is it?

Clown

I would you did but see how it chafes, how it rages,
how it takes up the shore—but that's not to the
point. O, the most piteous cry of the poor souls!

---

58 *would*: wish.
59 *youth*: young lads.

61 *wronging the ancientry*: upsetting the old folk.
62–3 *boiled brains*: hot-headed idiots.

66 *If . . . have them*: if I'm going to find them anywhere.
67 *browsing of*: grazing on.
   Good . . . will: send me good luck, if it be thy (i.e. God's) will.

69 *barne*: bairn, child; even in Shakespeare's day, the word was largely restricted to northern dialects.
   child: girl.
70 *scape*: escapade, naughtiness.
71 *bookish*: educated.
72–3 *stair-work . . . work*: The Shepherd suggests different means by which lovers (in fiction) have got access to their mistresses, and the places of their rendezvous—up the back stairs; by hiding in a trunk; lurking behind doors.
76 *hallowed*: hollered, shouted.
   but even: only just.

78 *to talk on*: that will be talked about.

83 *firmament*: heaven.
84 *bodkin*: needle.

87 *takes up*: swallows up.

90 *anon*: immediately.
91 *yeast*: foam.
92 *hogshead*: barrel of beer.
land-service: military (as opposed to naval) fighting.

96 *flap-dragoned it*: swallowed it as though it were a flap-dragon (= a raisin burning with brandy, whose flames were extinguished by quickly closing the mouth).

102 *winked*: blinked, closed my eyes.
107 *lacked footing*: had nothing to stand on—i.e. been useless.

111 *bearing-cloth*: christening-robe (the rich shawl in which a child is carried to church for baptism).

113–14 *It was . . . fairies*: the fairies foretold that I would be rich.
114–15 *some changeling*: child involved in a fairy baby-switch (usually when a beautiful human child is swapped by the fairies for an ugly fairy infant).
116 *made*: i.e. assured of future prosperity.
117 *you're . . . live*: you will live well for the rest of your life.
120 *close*: secret: to disclose the possession of fairy gifts would (it was believed) bring bad luck.
next: nearest.
121 *still*: always.

Sometimes to see 'em, and not to see 'em: now the
90 ship boring the moon with her mainmast, and anon swallowed with yeast and froth, as you'd thrust a cork into a hogshead. And then for the land-service: to see how the bear tore out his shoulder bone, how he cried to me for help, and said his name was
95 Antigonus, a nobleman. But to make an end of the ship: to see how the sea flap-dragoned it; but first, how the poor souls roared, and the sea mocked them; and how the poor gentleman roared, and the bear mocked him, both roaring louder than the sea or
100 weather.

Shepherd
Name of mercy, when was this, boy?

Clown
Now, now! I have not winked since I saw these sights. The men are not yet cold under water, nor the bear half dined on the gentleman; he's at it now.

Shepherd
105 Would I had been by, to have helped the old man!

Clown
I would you had been by the ship side, to have helped her: there your charity would have lacked footing.

Shepherd
Heavy matters, heavy matters! But look thee here, boy. Now bless thyself: thou met'st with things
110 dying, I with things new-born. Here's a sight for thee: look thee, a bearing-cloth for a squire's child! Look thee here!

He points to the box

Take up, take up, boy; open it. So, let's see. It was told me I should be rich by the fairies. This is some
115 changeling. Open't. What's within, boy?

Clown
[*Opening the box*] You're a made old man. If the sins of your youth are forgiven you, you're well to live. Gold! All gold!

Shepherd
This is fairy gold, boy, and 'twill prove so. Up with't,
120 keep it close. Home, home, the next way! We are lucky, boy, and to be so still requires nothing but

secrecy. Let my sheep go! Come, good boy, the next
way home.

Clown

Go you the next way with your findings. I'll go see if
125 the bear be gone from the gentleman, and how much
he hath eaten. They are never curst but when they
are hungry. If there be any of him left, I'll bury it.

Shepherd

That's a good deed. If thou mayst discern by that
which is left of him what he is, fetch me to th'sight of
130 him.

Clown

Marry will I; and you shall help to put him
i'th'ground.

Shepherd

'Tis a lucky day, boy, and we'll do good deeds on't.

[*Exeunt*

126 *curst*: bad-tempered, savage.

131 *Marry*: indeed (literally, 'by [the Virgin] Mary').

Act 4

Act 4 Scene 1

The Chorus is spoken by the personification of Time, traditionally presented as an old man with wings and an hourglass. His rhymed couplets stand distinct from the 'realistic' verse in the rest of the play.

1 *try*: test.
1–2 *both joy . . . bad*: a joy and a terror to good and bad alike.
2 *that*: he that.
 unfolds: reveals.
3 *in the name of*: with the authority of.
4 *use my wings*: i.e. fly past.
 crime: i.e. against the 'unity of time'; see line 8 *note*.
6–7 *leave . . . gap*: don't explain how matters have developed over such a long period.
8 *o'erthrow law*: The 'law' specifically referred to here is the ruling of Renaissance dramatic critics about the 'unity of time', which stipulated that the action of a play should be completed in a single day.
 one self-born hour: at one and the same hour to which Time himself has given birth.
9–11 *Let me . . . received*: accept me as the same now as I have always been, before the oldest tradition was established or that which is now in fashion.

Scene 1

Enter Time, *the* Chorus

> I that please some, try all; both joy and terror
> Of good and bad; that makes and unfolds error,
> Now take upon me, in the name of Time,
> To use my wings. Impute it not a crime
> 5 To me or my swift passage that I slide
> O'er sixteen years, and leave the growth untried
> Of that wide gap, since it is in my power
> To o'erthrow law, and in one self-born hour
> To plant and o'erwhelm custom. Let me pass
> 10 The same I am ere ancient'st order was
> Or what is now receiv'd. I witness to

13–15 *make stale . . . to it*: make this shining
moment seem as old-fashioned as my
story is nowadays.

15 *Your . . . allowing*: if you will be patient
and allow me.

16 *glass*: hour-glass.
   scene: play.

17 *As*: as if.

17–19 *Leontes . . . imagine me*: leaving
Leontes—who is grieving so much over
the results of his foolish ('fond')
jealousy that he has shut himself away
from everybody—picture me.

22 *I mention'd*: i.e. earlier in the play—
Time and the playwright are here
identified.

23 *pace*: hurry.

24 *in grace*: in beauty and favour.

25 *Equal with wond'ring*: just as much as all
the admiration she receives has grown.

26 *list not*: would rather not.

28 *after*: the *f* was probably not sounded,
making a rhyme for 'daughter'.

29 *argument*: theme, topic.

29–32 'Admit this, that you have wasted
time worse before now—and if you
haven't, then allow Time himself to
hope that you never will.'

The times that brought them in; so shall I do
To th'freshest things now reigning, and make stale
The glistering of this present, as my tale
15 Now seems to it. Your patience this allowing,
I turn my glass, and give my scene such growing
As you had slept between. Leontes leaving—
Th'effects of his fond jealousies so grieving
That he shuts up himself—imagine me,
20 Gentle spectators, that I now may be
In fair Bohemia; and remember well,
I mention'd a son o'th'king's, which Florizel
I now name to you; and with speed so pace
To speak of Perdita, now grown in grace
25 Equal with wond'ring. What of her ensues
I list not prophesy; but let Time's news
Be known when 'tis brought forth. A shepherd's
   daughter,
And what to her adheres, which follows after,
Is th'argument of Time. Of this allow,
30 If ever you have spent time worse ere now;
If never, yet that Time himself doth say
He wishes earnestly you never may.

[*Exit*

Act 4   Scene 2

The second part of the play opens, like the
first, with a scene in prose. We learn that
Camillo is homesick and wants to return to
Sicilia, but Polixenes will not hear of his
leaving Bohemia; and we are told that the
king's son, Florizel, is giving his father some
cause for anxiety.

1 *importunate*: demanding.

2–3 'It makes me ill to refuse you
anything, but it would kill me to grant
this request.'

5 *been aired abroad*: breathed the air of
foreign countries.

7 *feeling*: distressing.

8 *be some allay*: give some comfort.
  o'erween: flatter myself.

10 *As*: if.
   wipe not out: don't cancel out.

Scene 2

Enter Polixenes *and* Camillo

Polixenes

I pray thee, good Camillo, be no more importunate.
'Tis a sickness denying thee anything; a death to
grant this.

Camillo

It is fifteen years since I saw my country. Though I
5 have for the most part been aired abroad, I desire to
lay my bones there. Besides, the penitent king, my
master, hath sent for me; to whose feeling sorrows I
might be some allay—or I o'erween to think so—
which is another spur to my departure.

Polixenes

10 As thou lov'st me, Camillo, wipe not out the rest of
thy services by leaving me now. The need I have of

13 *thus to want thee*: to lose you like this.

14–15 *made me . . . them*: started off some projects for me which no one else can cope with.

17 *considered*: rewarded.

18–19 *to be . . . study*: I will try hard to think how I can show more gratitude.

19–20 *my profit . . . friendships*: what I shall get out of it will be still more friendly service.

21 *whose very naming*: just the name of it.

22 *as . . . him*: as you so rightly call him; it would seem that Leontes has made some attempt to propitiate Polixenes.

24 *are*: The plural 'queen and children' confuses the verb.

27 *issue*: children.
gracious: well-behaved.

28 *they have approved*: the children have shown.

30 *happier . . . be*: business may happen to be.

31 *missingly noted*: noticed by missing him—i.e. he has been conspicuously absent.
of late: recently.
much retired: often away from.

32 *less . . . exercises*: his royal highness does not spend as much time with his studies.

35 *I have . . . service*: I have spies watching him for me.

36 *his removedness*: where he has got to.

37 *intelligence*: information.

39 *very nothing*: nothing at all.

40 *unspeakable estate*: inestimable wealth.

42 *of most rare note*: most remarkable.

42–3 *the report . . . cottage*: the accounts that have been heard of her must come from some higher source than a peasant's home.

45 *angle*: fishing-hook, bait.

46–7 *not . . . we are*: i.e. in disguise.

47 *question*: talk.

thee thine own goodness hath made. Better not to have had thee than thus to want thee. Thou, having made me businesses which none without thee can
15 sufficiently manage, must either stay to execute them thyself or take away with thee the very services thou hast done; which, if I have not enough considered— as too much I cannot—to be more thankful to thee shall be my study, and my profit therein the heaping
20 friendships. Of that fatal country, Sicilia, prithee speak no more, whose very naming punishes me with the remembrance of that penitent, as thou call'st him, and reconciled king, my brother; whose loss of his most precious queen and children are even now to be
25 afresh lamented. Say to me, when saw'st thou the Prince Florizel, my son? Kings are no less unhappy, their issue not being gracious, than they are in losing them when they have approved their virtues.

Camillo

Sir, it is three days since I saw the prince. What his
30 happier affairs may be are to me unknown; but I have missingly noted he is of late much retired from court, and is less frequent to his princely exercises than formerly he hath appeared.

Polixenes

I have considered so much, Camillo, and with some
35 care; so far that I have eyes under my service which look upon his removedness, from whom I have this intelligence: that he is seldom from the house of a most homely shepherd—a man, they say, that from very nothing, and beyond the imagination of his
40 neighbours, is grown into an unspeakable estate.

Camillo

I have heard, sir, of such a man, who hath a daughter of most rare note: the report of her is extended more than can be thought to begin from such a cottage.

Polixenes

That's likewise part of my intelligence, but, I fear,
45 the angle that plucks our son thither. Thou shalt accompany us to the place, where we will, not appearing what we are, have some question with the shepherd; from whose simplicity I think it not uneasy to get the cause of my son's resort thither.

50 *be my present partner*: join with me now.

50 Prithee be my present partner in this business, and
lay aside the thoughts of Sicilia.
　　　　Camillo
I willingly obey your command.
　　　　Polixenes
My best Camillo! We must disguise ourselves.
　　　　　　　　　　　　　　　　　　[*Exeunt*

Act 4   Scene 3

A strange figure sings his way on to the stage
and introduces himself to the audience as
Autolycus. He encounters the Clown who is
on his way to market, and easily tricks him of
his money.

1–12 For music to the songs in this scene
　　　see Songs, p.128.
1　*peer*: appear, show through the earth.
2　*doxy*: beggar's wench.
3　*sweet o'the year*: best part of the year.
4　*pale*: confines, restraints *and also* pallor
　　(caused by the cold of winter).
5–8　'Linen spread out to dry sharpens my
　　appetite for stealing ('*pugging*') and the
　　drink (bought with money from the
　　stolen sheets) will be fit for a king.'
11　*aunts*: wenches, 'doxies'—see line 2.
14　*three-pile*: thick, costly velvet.
　　am out of service: have got the sack.
15–18　'Why should I get upset about that?
　　When the moon is shining and I am
　　roaming around (looking for things to
　　steal), I'm doing what is right for me.'
19–22　'Since tinkers can carry leather tool-
　　bags around with them, then I shall be
　　able to explain myself away even if they
　　put me in the stocks.' Autolycus is
　　probably carrying a hold-all for his loot!
　　Tradesmen were permitted to travel
　　freely around the countryside, but
　　vagabonds were punished with whips
　　and the stocks.
23–4　*My traffic . . . linen*: I deal only in
　　sheets—keep an eye on smaller articles
　　when the kite is building a nest (which
　　can be lined with stolen scraps of fabric
　　etc.).

Scene 3

Enter Autolycus, *singing*

Autolycus
　　　When daffodils begin to peer,
　　　　With heigh, the doxy over the dale,
　　　Why, then comes in the sweet o'the year,
　　　　For the red blood reigns in the winter's
　　　　　pale.

5

　　　The white sheet bleaching on the hedge,
　　　　With heigh, the sweet birds O, how
　　　　　they sing!
　　　Doth set my pugging tooth an edge,
　　　　For a quart of ale is a dish for a king.

10

　　　The lark, that tirra-lyra chants,
　　　　With heigh, with heigh, the thrush and
　　　　　the jay,
　　　Are summer songs for me and my aunts
　　　　While we lie tumbling in the hay.

24 *Autolycus*: This was the name given, in classical mythology, to the son of Mercury, patron of thieves and pickpockets.

24–5 *being . . . Mercury*: was born, just like me, under the sign of Mercury.

26 *die and drab*: gambling and women. *purchased*: brought me.

27 *caparison*: get-up. *my revenue*: I get my living from. *silly cheat*: petty trickery, *or*, tricking the simple-minded.

28 *Gallows . . . highway*: threats of death and thrashing are powerful deterrents against being a highwayman.

29–30 *For the life . . . of it*: as for the future (*or* 'any life hereafter'), I never give it a thought.

31 *every . . . tods*: every eleven sheep yield a tod (= 28 lb./12.7 kgs) of wool.

32 *pound . . . shilling*: i.e. 21 shillings (105p).

34 *If . . . hold*: if the trap works. *cock*: woodcock (proverbially a foolish bird that could easily be caught in a trap).

35 *counters*: counting-discs (the earliest kind of calculator).

36 *to buy*: For the items on the Clown's shopping-list the 1611 prices would have been: sugar 7p. lb.; currants 2½p. lb.; rice 3p. lb.; saffron 25p. oz.; mace 80p. lb.; nutmegs 30p. lb.; ginger 26p. lb.; prunes 1½p. lb.; raisins 5p. lb.

39 *lays it on*: makes the most of it.

40 *me*: The word is used here simply as an intensifier.

41 *three-man-song men*: singers of three-part songs for male voices (usually treble, tenor, and bass).

42 *means*: medium-range singers, tenors; the Clown makes a pun with 'good . . . mean . . . base'. *but one Puritan*: there's only one Puritan (who presumably takes the treble part). Puritans, much ridiculed in Elizabethan drama, were said to sing with a high, nasal sound.

43 *to hornpipes*: even to the music of hornpipes. The hornpipe used for country dances was a shrill-sounding instrument which could be used to play the treble part when a singer was lacking.

I have served Prince Florizel, and in my time wore three-pile; but now I am out of service.

15   But shall I go mourn for that, my dear?
            The pale moon shines by night:
         And when I wander here and there
            I then do most go right.

         If tinkers may have leave to live,
20   And bear the sow-skin budget,
         Then my account I well may give,
            And in the stocks avouch it.

My traffic is sheets; when the kite builds, look to lesser linen. My father named me Autolycus, who, being, as I
25 am, littered under Mercury, was likewise a snapper-up of unconsidered trifles. With die and drab I purchased this caparison, and my revenue is the silly cheat. Gallows and knock are too powerful on the highway: beating and hanging are terrors to me. For the life to
30 come, I sleep out the thought of it. A prize! A prize!

Enter Clown

Clown
Let me see: every 'leven wether tods, every tod yields pound and odd shilling; fifteen hundred shorn, what comes the wool to?

Autolycus
[*Aside*] If the springe hold, the cock's mine.

Clown
35 I cannot do't without counters. Let me see: what am I to buy for our sheep-shearing feast? Three pound of sugar, five pound of currants, rice—what will this sister of mine do with rice? But my father hath made her mistress of the feast, and she lays it on. She hath
40 made me four-and-twenty nosegays for the shearers, three-man-song men all, and very good ones; but they are most of them means and basses—but one Puritan amongst them, and he sings psalms to hornpipes. I must have saffron to colour the warden pies; mace;
45 dates—none, that's out of my note; nutmegs, seven; a race or two of ginger, but that I may beg; four

44 *warden pies*: pies made with warden
    pears.
    mace: spice made of the outer covering
    of the nutmeg.
45 *out of my note*: crossed off my list.
46 *race*: root.
47 *o'th'sun*: sun-dried.
49 No other instance of this exclamation
    has been found.
50 *Pluck but off*: just pull off.

55 *stripes*: beating.

62 *horseman*: highwayman.
    footman: footpad, mugger.

64 *should*: must.
    by: to judge by; a highwayman's coat
    would be of better quality than that of a
    lowly footpad.
66 *hot service*: heavy use.

70 *softly*: gently.

pounds of prunes, and as many of raisins o'th'sun.

Autolycus

[*Grovelling on the ground*] O that ever I was born!

Clown

I'th'name of me!

Autolycus

50 O, help me, help me! Pluck but off these rags; and
then death, death!

Clown

Alack, poor soul! Thou hast need of more rags to lay
on thee, rather than have these off.

Autolycus

O sir, the loathsomeness of them offend me more
55 than the stripes I have received, which are mighty
ones and millions.

Clown

Alas, poor man! A million of beating may come to a
great matter.

Autolycus

I am robbed, sir, and beaten; my money and apparel
60 ta'en from me, and these detestable things put upon
me.

Clown

What, by a horseman or a footman?

Autolycus

A footman, sweet sir, a footman.

Clown

Indeed, he should be a footman, by the garments he
65 has left with thee. If this be a horseman's coat, it hath
seen very hot service. Lend me thy hand, I'll help
thee. Come, lend me thy hand.

He helps him up

Autolycus

O, good sir, tenderly, O!

Clown

Alas, poor soul!

Autolycus

70 O, good sir, softly, good sir! I fear, sir, my shoulder-
blade is out.

Clown

How now? Canst stand?

Autolycus

Softly, dear sir; [*He picks his pockets*] good sir, softly.
You ha'done me a charitable office.

Clown

75 Dost lack any money? I have a little money for thee.

Autolycus

No, good, sweet sir; no, I beseech you, sir. I have a
kinsman not past three-quarters of a mile hence,
unto whom I was going. I shall there have money, or
anything I want. Offer me no money, I pray you:
80 that kills my heart.

Clown

What manner of fellow was he that robbed you?

Autolycus

A fellow, sir, that I have known to go about with
troll-my-dames. I knew him once a servant of the
prince. I cannot tell, good sir, for which of his
85 virtues it was, but he was certainly whipped out of
the court.

Clown

His vices, you would say. There's no virtue whipped
out of the court: they cherish it to make it stay there;
and yet it will no more but abide.

Autolycus

90 Vices I would say, sir. I know this man well. He hath
been since an ape-bearer; then a process-server, a
bailiff; then he compassed a motion of the Prodigal
Son, and married a tinker's wife within a mile where
my land and living lies; and having flown over many
95 knavish professions, he settled only in rogue. Some
call him Autolycus.

Clown

Out upon him! Prig, for my life, prig! He haunts
wakes, fairs, and bear-baitings.

Autolycus

Very true, sir; he, sir, he: that's the rogue that put me
100 into this apparel.

Clown

Not a more cowardly rogue in all Bohemia. If you
had but looked big and spit at him, he'd have run.

Autolycus

I must confess to you, sir, I am no fighter. I am false

77 *past*: more than.

83 *troll-my-dames*: no-good women.
Autolycus coins a phrase from 'troll' (=
'cruise in search of sexual partners')
and 'troll-madam', a game in which
balls were rolled through hoops on a
board.
once: at one time.

89 *but abide*: only stay a little while.

91 *ape-bearer*: travelling showman with a
monkey.
process-server: bearer of legal writs; the
parenthetical 'a bailiff' was probably
intended as an alternative.
92 *compassed*: got hold of, and went around
with.
motion: puppet-show; usually these
demonstrated stories from the Bible.
92–3 *the Prodigal Son*: This story is told in
Luke 15: 11–32.
94 *living*: estate.
flown over: tried his hand at.
95 *in rogue*: for being a rogue.
97 *Prig*: thief.
haunts: hangs around.
98 *wakes*: popular holiday festivals.

102 *big*: fierce.

103–4 *false of heart*: faint-hearted.

of heart that way, and that he knew, I warrant
105 him.
           Clown
     How do you now?
           Autolycus
     Sweet sir, much better than I was: I can stand and
     walk. I will even take my leave of you, and pace softly
     towards my kinsman's.
           Clown
110 Shall I bring thee on the way?
           Autolycus
     No, good-faced sir; no, sweet sir.
           Clown
     Then fare thee well. I must go buy spices for our
     sheep-shearing.
           Autolycus
     Prosper you, sweet sir!   [*Exit* Clown
115 Your purse is not hot enough to purchase your spice.
     I'll be with you at your sheep-shearing too. If I make
     not this cheat bring out another, and the shearers
     prove sheep, let me be unrolled, and my name put in
     the book of virtue!
120   [*Sings*] Jog on, jog on, the footpath way,
                 And merrily hent the stile-a:
              A merry heart goes all the day,
                 Your sad tires in a mile-a.
                                              [*Exit*

110 *bring thee*: keep you company.

115 *not hot enough*: The Clown cannot buy
     his hot spices with a cold (= empty)
     purse.
117 *cheat*: profitable deception.
     bring out: lead on to.
118 *unrolled*: struck off the roll (of the
     fraternity of rogues and vagabonds).

121 *hent*: grab hold of.

Act 4   Scene 4

Whilst the country folk are assembling to celebrate their sheepshearing festival, the audience's attention is focused on a lover and his lass—Florizel and Perdita. Strangers join the company, where they are welcomed with flowers, and stand by whilst the pedlar entertains with his songs and patter. In a solemn moment Florizel declares his firm intent to make Perdita his wife—a proposal which is received with joy by the Shepherd, but not by one of the strangers, who casts off his disguise and reveals himself as Florizel's outraged father, Polixenes. The lovers are thrown into despair, but Camillo (the other disguised stranger) has a scheme to solve all problems. Autolycus is enlisted to help the lovers escape, and when Camillo has escorted Florizel and Perdita off the stage Autolycus remains to overhear a conversation between the Shepherd and his son. Once again Autolycus supplies some very necessary aid.

1 *weeds*: garments.
2 *give a life*: make you a different character.
   Flora: the goddess (in classical mythology) of springtime, who was traditionally represented with a crown of flowers.
3 *Peering . . . front*: as she appears at the beginning of April.
4 *as*: like.
   petty gods: minor rural deities attending Flora.
6 *extremes*: extravagances.
8 *mark o'th'land*: focus for every eye in the country.
9 *swain's wearing*: the clothes of a peasant.
10 *prank'd*: decked, decorated.
   But that: if it were not that.
11 *In every mess*: at every sitting.
12 *Digest*: enjoy, relish.
   with accustom: as being customary.
14 *show myself a glass*: look at myself in a mirror.
16 *Jove . . . cause*: may Jupiter—king of the gods—give you some good reason for talking like this.
17 *difference*: i.e. in social status.
17–18 *your . . . fear*: someone in your high position does not know what it is to be afraid.

Scene 4

Enter Florizel *and* Perdita

Florizel
These your unusual weeds to each part of you
Does give a life: no shepherdess, but Flora
Peering in April's front. This your sheep-shearing
Is as a meeting of the petty gods,
5 And you the queen on't.

Perdita
                              Sir, my gracious lord,
To chide at your extremes it not becomes me—
O, pardon that I name them: your high self,
The gracious mark o'th'land, you have obscur'd
With a swain's wearing, and me, poor lowly maid,
10 Most goddess-like prank'd up. But that our feasts
In every mess have folly, and the feeders
Digest it with accustom, I should blush
To see you so attir'd, swoon, I think,
To show myself a glass.
Florizel
                              I bless the time
15 When my good falcon made her flight across
Thy father's ground.
Perdita
                              Now Jove afford you cause!
To me the difference forges dread; your greatness
Hath not been us'd to fear. Even now I tremble

21–2 *his work . . . bound up*: his noble son
in this ridiculous get-up (like a good
book with cheap covers).

22 *Vilely*: meanly, wretchedly.

23 *flaunts*: fancy clothes.

24 *Apprehend*: look forward to, expect.

25–30 *The gods . . . swain*: The prince (in
lines inspired by *Pandosto*) refers to
stories told by Ovid in his
Metamorphoses, a book popular among
the Elizabethans and frequently cited by
Shakespeare. Jupiter, the most powerful
of the gods, became a bull in order to
seduce Europa; Neptune changed
himself into a ram to take Theophane;
and Apollo the sun-god ('fire-rob'd')
served as a shepherd.

31 *transformations*: metamorphoses.

32 *piece*: person.

33 *in . . . chaste*: with such an innocent
intention.

38 'One of these two things must happen.'

40 *I my life*: Perdita will have to change her
way of life—or even give up her life.

41 *forc'd*: unnatural.

42–3 *Or . . . Or . . .*: either . . . or . . .

43–4 *I cannot . . . any*: I shall be no good to
myself or to anybody else.

46 *Though . . . no*: whatever fate may do to
prevent me.

48 *the while*: right now.

49 *Lift up your countenance*: let's see you
smile.

50 *nuptial*: wedding.

52 *auspicious*: favourable.

To think your father by some accident
20 Should pass this way, as you did. O, the Fates!
How would he look to see his work, so noble,
Vilely bound up? What would he say? Or how
Should I, in these my borrowed flaunts, behold
The sternness of his presence?

Florizel
                                        Apprehend
25 Nothing but jollity. The gods themselves,
Humbling their deities to love, have taken
The shapes of beasts upon them: Jupiter
Became a bull, and bellow'd; the green Neptune
A ram, and bleated; and the fire-rob'd god,
30 Golden Apollo, a poor, humble swain,
As I seem now. Their transformations
Were never for a piece of beauty rarer,
Nor in a way so chaste, since my desires
Run not before mine honour, nor my lusts
35 Burn hotter than my faith.

Perdita
                                  O, but sir,
Your resolution cannot hold when 'tis
Oppos'd, as it must be, by th'power of the king.
One of these two must be necessities,
Which then will speak: that you must change this
    purpose
40 Or I my life.

Florizel
            Thou dearest Perdita,
With these forc'd thoughts, I prithee, darken not
The mirth o'th'feast. Or I'll be thine, my fair,
Or not my father's. For I cannot be
Mine own, nor anything to any, if
45 I be not thine. To this I am most constant,
Though destiny say no. Be merry, gentle;
Strangle such thoughts as these with anything
That you behold the while. Your guests are coming:
Lift up your countenance as it were the day
50 Of celebration of that nuptial which
We two have sworn shall come.

Perdita
                              O lady Fortune,
Stand you auspicious!

Florizel
　　　　　　　　　　　　　　　See, your guests approach.
Address yourself to entertain them sprightly,
And let's be red with mirth.

Enter Shepherd, *with* Polixenes *and*
Camillo *disguised*; Clown, Mopsa, Dorcas,
and others

53　'Get yourself ready to give them a
　　hearty welcome.'

Shepherd
55　Fie, daughter! When my old wife liv'd, upon
　　This day she was both pantler, butler, cook;
　　Both dame and servant; welcom'd all, serv'd all;
　　Would sing her song and dance her turn; now here,
　　At upper end o'th'table, now i'th'middle;
60　On his shoulder, and his; her face o'fire
　　With labour, and the thing she took to quench it
　　She would to each one sip. You are retired,
　　As if you were a feasted one and not
　　The hostess of the meeting. Pray you, bid
65　These unknown friends to's welcome, for it is
　　A way to make us better friends, more known.
　　Come, quench your blushes and present yourself
　　That which you are, Mistress o'th'Feast. Come on,
　　And bid us welcome to your sheep-shearing,
70　As your good flock shall prosper.
　　Perdita
　　[*To* Polixenes]　　　　　　　　　Sir, welcome.
　　It is my father's will I should take on me
　　The hostess-ship o'th'day. [*To* Camillo] You're
　　　　welcome, sir.
　　Give me those flowers there, Dorcas. Reverend sirs,

56　*pantler*: servant in charge of the pantry.
　　butler: servant in charge of the wine
　　cellar.
57　*dame*: mistress in charge of the
　　household.
60　*On his . . . his*: leaning over the shoulder
　　of first one man and then another.
61　*thing*: i.e. drink.
62　*sip*: drink as a toast.
63　*a feasted one*: one of those—the
　　shepherds and shepherdesses—for
　　whom the feast is given.
66　*more known*: once we know who they
　　are.
73　*those flowers*: Perdita distributes her
　　floral tributes according to the time-
　　honoured 'language of flowers'.

74 *rosemary and rue*: These signify
respectively 'remembrance' (i.e. of
friendship) and 'grace' (repentance).

75 *Seeming and savour*: appearance and
scent.

82 *gillyvors*: pinks; the streaks are caused
by hybridization—cross-breeding two
different strains of flower.

84 *care not*: would rather not.

85 *slips*: cuttings.

86 *For*: because.

87 *art*: artifice.

88 *great creating Nature*: Here, and at many
other times in the play, Nature is
presented as a divine power (and given
the appropriate capital letter).

89–90 *Nature is . . . that mean*: i.e. every
man-made means of improving on the
works of Nature has itself been made by
Nature.

93 *scion*: offshoot.

For you there's rosemary and rue; these keep
75 Seeming and savour all the winter long:
Grace and remembrance be to you both,
And welcome to our shearing!
   Polixenes
                        Shepherdess—
A fair one are you—well you fit our ages
With flowers of winter.
   Perdita
                   Sir, the year growing ancient,
80 Not yet on summer's death nor on the birth
Of trembling winter, the fairest flowers o'th'season
Are our carnations and streak'd gillyvors,
Which some call Nature's bastards; of that kind
Our rustic garden's barren, and I care not
85 To get slips of them.
   Polixenes
               Wherefore, gentle maiden,
Do you neglect them?
   Perdita
                For I have heard it said
There is an art which in their piedness shares
With great creating Nature.
   Polixenes
              Say there be;
Yet Nature is made better by no mean
90 But Nature makes that mean; so over that art
Which you say adds to Nature is an art
That Nature makes. You see, sweet maid, we marry
A gentler scion to the wildest stock,
And make conceive a bark of baser kind
95 By bud of nobler race. This is an art
Which does mend Nature—change it, rather—but
The art itself is Nature.
   Perdita
              So it is.
   Polixenes
Then make your garden rich in gillyvors,
And do not call them bastards.
   Perdita
                  I'll not put
100 The dibble in earth to set one slip of them:
No more than, were I painted, I would wish

104 *Hot lavender*: Herbs were divided into 'cold' (those which flowered early) and 'hot'.

106 *weeping*: i.e. wet with dew.

116 *Proserpina*: The daughter of Ceres (classical goddess of corn and harvest) who was carried away by the god of the underworld whilst she was gathering flowers.

118 *Dis*: The same god was known as Pluto in Roman mythology.
    wagon: chariot.

121 *Juno*: queen of the gods.

122 *Cytherea*: Venus, the goddess of love.

122–5 *pale primroses . . . maids*: Primroses flower in the early spring, before the sun has reached its summer height. Their pale green-yellow colour suggests the anaemic pallor of some young girls, who were said to suffer from 'green-sickness'.

124 *Phoebus*: Phoebus Apollo, god of the sun.

This youth should say 'twere well, and only therefore
Desire to breed by me. Here's flowers for you:
Hot lavender, mints, savory, marjoram;
105 The marigold, that goes to bed wi' th' sun
And with him rises weeping; these are flowers
Of middle summer, and I think they are given
To men of middle age. Y'are very welcome.

Camillo
I should leave grazing, were I of your flock,
110 And only live by gazing.

Perdita
                              Out, alas!
You'd be so lean that blasts of January
Would blow you through and through. [*To* Florizel]
    Now, my fair'st friend,
I would I had some flowers o'th'spring, that might
Become your time of day—[*To the* Shepherdesses]
    and yours, and yours,
115 That wear upon your virgin branches yet
Your maidenheads growing. O Proserpina,
For the flowers now that, frighted, thou let'st fall
From Dis's wagon! Daffodils,
That come before the swallow dares, and take
120 The winds of March with beauty; violets, dim,
But sweeter than the lids of Juno's eyes
Or Cytherea's breath; pale primroses,
That die unmarried ere they can behold
Bright Phoebus in his strength—a malady

125 *oxlips*: These are larger and stronger than cowslips, and stand out boldly.

126 *crown imperial*: tall yellow fritillary.

127 *flower-de-luce*: fleur-de-lys, iris (often classed as a lily).

130 *Love*: Cupid, the god of love.

131 *or if*: i.e. if he is to be covered with flowers.

132 *quick*: alive.

134 *Whitsun pastorals*: country festivities held at Whitsuntide (e.g. May Day celebrations with morris-dancing and 'Robin Hood' plays).

136 *what is done*: what you have just been doing.

125 Most incident to maids; bold oxlips and
The crown imperial; lilies of all kinds,
The flower-de-luce being one: O, these I lack
To make you garlands of, and my sweet friend
To strew him o'er and o'er!

Florizel

What, like a corse?

Perdita

130 No, like a bank for Love to lie and play on,
Not like a corse; or if, not to be buried,
But quick and in mine arms. Come, take your flowers.
Methinks I play as I have seen them do
In Whitsun pastorals: sure this robe of mine
135 Does change my disposition.

Florizel

What you do
Still betters what is done. When you speak, sweet,
I'd have you do it ever; when you sing,
I'd have you buy and sell so, so give alms,
Pray so, and, for the ord'ring your affairs,
140 To sing them too; when you do dance, I wish you
A wave o'th'sea, that you might ever do
Nothing but that—move still, still so,

143 *own*: have.
143–6 *Each . . . queens*: every single act of
       yours, done in some special way which
       is all your own, is more perfect than the
       last one, and crowns what has gone
       before.
146 *Doricles*: The name that Florizel has
       assumed in his disguise as a shepherd.
147 *large*: lavish.
       But that: if it were not for the fact that.
148 *true*: noble, honourable.
149 *give you out*: proclaim you to be.

151 *the false way*: with an ulterior motive.
152 *skill*: reason, cause.
153 *put you to't*: give you cause to be afraid.
154 *turtles*: turtle doves (which were believed
       to mate for life).
155 *I'll . . . 'em*: I'll be sworn they do.

158 *smacks*: has a touch.

160 *makes . . . out*: brings a blush to her
       cheeks.
161 *curds and cream*: a kind of creamy
       custard, with clotted cream.

163 *Mopsa . . . mistress*: so Mopsa's your
       girl-friend now.
163–4 *garlic . . . with*: give her some garlic to
       sweeten her breath when she's kissing
       you.
165 *in good time*: oh yeah (an exclamation of
       contemptuous dismissal).
166 *we stand . . . manners*: we're on our best
       behaviour.

And own no other function. Each your doing,
So singular in each particular,
145 Crowns what you are doing in the present deeds,
That all your acts are queens.
       Perdita
                                    O Doricles,
Your praises are too large. But that your youth
And the true blood which peeps fairly through't
Do plainly give you out an unstain'd shepherd,
150 With wisdom I might fear, my Doricles,
You wooed me the false way.
       Florizel
                          I think you have
As little skill to fear as I have purpose
To put you to't. But come, our dance, I pray.
Your hand, my Perdita: so turtles pair,
155 That never mean to part.
       Perdita
                          I'll swear for 'em.
       Polixenes
This is the prettiest low-born lass that ever
Ran on the greensward: nothing she does or seems
But smacks of something greater than herself,
Too noble for this place.
       Camillo
                          He tells her something
160 That makes her blood look out. Good sooth, she is
The queen of curds and cream.
       Clown
Come on, strike up!
       Dorcas
Mopsa must be your mistress. Marry, garlic to mend
her kissing with!
       Mopsa
165 Now, in good time!
       Clown
Not a word, a word: we stand upon our manners.
Come, strike up!

       Music. A dance of Shepherds *and*
       Shepherdesses

170 *boasts himself*: and he claims.
171 *have . . . feeding*: come from a good home.
172 *his own report*: his own word for it.
173 *like sooth*: as though this is true.
178 *another*: the other.
    featly: gracefully.
181 *light upon her*: succeed, make a match with her.
183 *at the door*: This suggests that the feast is being held indoors.
184 *tabor and pipe*: The instruments—a small drum and a whistle-pipe or fife—played for morris-dancing.
185 *several*: different.
186 *tell*: count.
187 *ballads*: These were not only the popular songs of the day but also the equivalent of the tabloid newspapers, reporting current events and describing wonderful happenings (which are parodied below).
    grew to: were glued to.

Polixenes
Pray, good shepherd, what fair swain is this
Which dances with your daughter?
    Shepherd
170 They call him Doricles, and boasts himself
To have a worthy feeding; but I have it
Upon his own report and I believe it:
He looks like sooth. He says he loves my daughter.
I think so too; for never gazed the moon
175 Upon the water as he'll stand and read,
As 'twere, my daughter's eyes; and, to be plain,
I think there is not half a kiss to choose
Who loves another best.
    Polixenes
                                        She dances featly.
    Shepherd
So she does anything—though I report it,
180 That should be silent. If young Doricles
Do light upon her, she shall bring him that
Which he not dreams of.

                    Enter Servant

    Servant
O master, if you did but hear the pedlar at the door,
you would never dance again after a tabor and pipe;
185 no, the bagpipe could not move you. He sings several
tunes faster than you'll tell money; he utters them as
he had eaten ballads and all men's ears grew to his
tunes.

189 *better*: at a better time.
190–2 *but even . . . lamentably*: just as well whether it's a pathetic story sung to a jolly tune, or a funny story with a mournful melody. The Clown's enthusiasm confuses his vocabulary.

    Clown
He could never come better; he shall come in. I love
190 a ballad but even too well, if it be doleful matter
merrily set down; or a very pleasant thing indeed,
and sung lamentably.

193 *sizes*: kinds, tastes.

194 *milliner*: haberdasher (literally, a dealer in goods from Milan).

195 *without bawdry*: with no dirty meanings—but the 'delicate burdens' (= refrains) are all from bawdy songs.

196-7 *dildos and fadings*: These apparently harmless and meaningless words have acquired sexual overtones through repetition in bawdy songs (= 'artificial penis' and 'comings').

199 *break . . . gap*: break off his singing for a dirty joke (e.g. in a rhyming word or with a suggestive gesture).
he: i.e. the ballad-singer (or the writer).

200-1 *Whoop . . . man*: The refrain of a well-known ballad.

203 *brave*: fine, splendid.

204 *admirable conceited*: wonderfully inventive.

205 *unbraided*: not shop-soiled.

207 *points*: laces with fancy tags (for attaching the hose to the doublet); the Clown makes a pun on 'points' = legal details.

209 *by th'gross*: wholesale.
inkles: linen tapes.
caddisses: caddis-ribbons—worsted tapes used for garters.
cambrics, lawns: delicate fabrics for dressmaking.

210 *as*: as though.

212 *sleevehand*: wristband or cuff of a sleeve.
square: square piece of material covering the breast.

216 *You have of*: there are some of.

218 *go about to*: wish to.

218s.d. *singing*: Autolycus chants his wares in a typical pedlar's song.

Servant

He hath songs for man or woman, of all sizes: no milliner can so fit his customers with gloves. He has
195 the prettiest love-songs for maids; so without bawdry, which is strange; with such delicate burdens of dildos and fadings, jump her and thump her; and where some stretch-mouthed rascal would, as it were, mean mischief, and break a foul gap into the matter, he
200 makes the maid to answer, 'Whoop, do me no harm, good man'; puts him off, slights him with 'Whoop, do me no harm, good man'.

Polixenes

This is a brave fellow.

Clown

Believe me, thou talk'st of an admirable conceited
205 fellow. Has he any unbraided wares?

Servant

He hath ribbons of all the colours i'th'rainbow; points more than all the lawyers in Bohemia can learnedly handle, though they come to him by th'gross; inkles, caddisses, cambrics, lawns. Why, he
210 sings 'em over as they were gods or goddesses; you would think a smock were a she-angel, he so chants to the sleevehand and the work about the square on't.

Clown

Prithee bring him in, and let him approach singing.

Perdita

Forewarn him that he use no scurrilous words in's
215 tunes.

[*Exit* Servant

Clown

You have of these pedlars that have more in them than you'd think, sister.

Perdita

Ay, good brother, or go about to think.

Enter Autolycus, *singing*

Autolycus
Lawn as white as driven snow;
220   Cypress black as e'er was crow;
Gloves as sweet as damask roses;
Masks for faces, and for noses;
Bugle-bracelet, necklace-amber;
Perfume for a lady's chamber;
225   Golden coifs and stomachers
For my lads to give their dears;
Pins and poking-sticks of steel;
What maids lack from head to heel
Come buy of me, come, come buy, come buy;
230   Buy, lads, or else your lasses cry: Come buy.
Clown
If I were not in love with Mopsa, thou shouldst take
no money of me; but being enthralled as I am, it will
also be the bondage of certain ribbons and gloves.
Mopsa
I was promised them against the feast, but they come
235   not too late now.
Dorcas
He hath promised you more than that, or there be
liars.

220 *Cypress*: crape (used for funerals).

221 Gloves at this time were usually perfumed.

222 *Masks*: These were commonly worn by ladies as protection against the sun.

223 *Bugle-bracelet*: bracelet made with threaded bugle (= black glass) beads.

225 *coifs*: tight-fitting caps for ladies. *stomachers*: stiffened centre panels for ladies' dresses.

227 *poking-sticks of steel*: rods used to stiffen the starched ruffs.

232 *enthralled*: captivated, in bondage.

233 *bondage*: condition of being tied up (into a parcel).

234 *against*: in time for.

Mopsa

He hath paid you all he promised you; may be he has paid you more, which will shame you to give him 240 again.

Clown

Is there no manners left among maids? Will they wear their plackets where they should bear their faces? Is there not milking-time, when you are going to bed, or kiln-hole, to whistle of these secrets, but 245 you must be tittle-tattling before all our guests? 'Tis well they are whisp'ring. Clamor your tongues, and not a word more.

Mopsa

I have done. Come, you promised me a tawdry-lace and a pair of sweet gloves.

Clown

250 Have I not told thee how I was cozened by the way and lost all my money?

Autolycus

And indeed, sir, there are cozeners abroad: therefore it behoves men to be wary.

Clown

Fear not thou, man; thou shalt lose nothing here.

Autolycus

255 I hope so, sir, for I have about me many parcels of charge.

Clown

What hast here? Ballads?

Mopsa

Pray now, buy some. I love a ballad in print a-life, for then we are sure they are true.

Autolycus

260 Here's one to a very doleful tune, how a usurer's wife was brought to bed of twenty money-bags at a burden, and how she longed to eat adders' heads and toads carbonadoed.

Mopsa

Is it true, think you?

Autolycus

265 Very true, and but a month old.

Dorcas

Bless me from marrying a usurer!

241-3 *Will they . . . faces*: will they show everything they ought to hide; *plackets* = petticoat pockets or openings—and consequently the private parts concealed by the petticoat.

244 *kiln-hole*: the fire-hole of a kiln, warm and cosy for gossiping.
whistle of: divulge, whisper about.

246 *Clamor*: clam up, shut up.

248 *tawdry-lace*: brightly coloured scarf (so called from the fairs held on St Audrey's day; the saint had interpreted the tumour in her throat as punishment for her vanity in wearing fancy handkerchiefs round her neck).

249 *sweet*: perfumed.
250 *cozened*: swindled.
253 *it behoves men*: it's necessary for people.
255-6 *parcels of charge*: valuable goods.
258 *a-life*: upon my life, dearly.
261 *brought to bed*: gave birth.
261-2 *at a burden*: all at once.

263 *carbonadoed*: cut across and broiled.

267 *to't*: as witness to it.

269 *abroad*: around the country.

272 *anon*: presently.

273 *ballad, of a fish*: Ballads describing monstrous fishes were entered for publication in the Stationers Register in April and May 1604.

278 *exchange flesh*: have sex.

281 *Five . . . at it*: certified by five justices of the peace.

286 *passing*: extremely.
287 *the tune*: Autolycus's ballads provide new lyrics for existing hit tunes.

294 *Have at it*: let's have a go at it.

Autolycus
Here's the midwife's name to't: one Mistress Taleporter, and five or six honest wives that were present. Why should I carry lies abroad?

Mopsa
270 Pray you now, buy it.

Clown
Come on, lay it by, and let's first see more ballads; we'll buy the other things anon.

Autolycus
Here's another ballad, of a fish that appeared upon the coast on Wednesday the fourscore of April, forty
275 thousand fathom above water, and sung this ballad against the hard hearts of maids. It was thought she was a woman, and was turned into a cold fish for she would not exchange flesh with one that loved her. The ballad is very pitiful, and as true.

Dorcas
280 Is it true too, think you?

Autolycus
Five justices' hands at it, and witnesses more than my pack will hold.

Clown
Lay it by too. Another.

Autolycus
This is a merry ballad, but a very pretty one.

Mopsa
285 Let's have some merry ones.

Autolycus
Why, this is a passing merry one, and goes to the tune of 'Two maids wooing a man'. There's scarce a maid westward but she sings it; 'tis in request, I can tell you.

Mopsa
290 We can both sing it. If thou'lt bear a part, thou shalt hear; 'tis in three parts.

Dorcas
We had the tune on't a month ago.

Autolycus
I can bear my part: you must know 'tis my occupation. Have at it with you.

They sing

Autolycus

295   Get you hence, for I must go.
         Where it fits not you to know.

Dorcas
         Whither?

Mopsa
                    O whither?

Dorcas
                              Whither?

Mopsa
         It becomes thy oath full well
         Thou to me thy secrets tell.

Dorcas

300   Me too; let me go thither.

Mopsa
         Or thou go'st to th'grange or mill.

Dorcas
         If to either, thou dost ill.

Autolycus
         Neither.

Dorcas
                    What, neither?

Autolycus
                              Neither.

Dorcas
         Thou hast sworn my love to be.

Mopsa

305   Thou hast sworn it more to me.
Then whither go'st? Say, whither?

Clown

We'll have this song out anon by ourselves: my father
and the gentlemen are in sad talk, and we'll not
trouble them. Come, bring away thy pack after me.

310   Wenches, I'll buy for you both. Pedlar, let's have the
first choice. Follow me, girls.

[*Exit with* Dorcas *and* Mopsa

Autolycus

And you shall pay well for 'em.

He follows them, singing

Will you buy any tape,
Or lace for your cape,

315   My dainty duck, my dear-a?
Any silk, any thread,
Any toys for your head,
Of the new'st and fin'st, fin'st wear-a?
Come to the pedlar:

320   Money's a meddler
That doth utter all men's ware-a.

[*Exit*

Enter Servant

Servant

Master, there is three carters, three shepherds, three
neat-herds, three swine-herds, that have made
themselves all men of hair: they call themselves

325   Saltiers, and they have a dance which the wenches
say is a gallimaufry of gambols, because they are not
in't; but they themselves are o'th'mind, if it be not
too rough for some that know little but bowling, it
will please plentifully.

Shepherd

330   Away! We'll none on't: here has been too much
homely foolery already. I know, sir, we weary you.

Polixenes

You weary those that refresh us. Pray, let's see these
four threes of herdsmen.

307 *have . . . anon*: finish this song
presently.
308 *sad*: serious.

317 *toys*: bits and pieces.

320–1 'Money comes into everything, and
keeps everything in circulation.'
323 *neat-herds*: cowherds.
324 *made themselves . . . hair*: the men have
disguised themselves as satyrs.
325 *Saltiers*: The Servant's mistaking of
'satyrs'—or else a name for the group
suggesting special skills in jumping.

326 *gallimaufry*: mixture, medley.
327 *o'th'mind*: have the intention.
328 *bowling*: i.e. quiet, slow-moving games.
333 *threes*: trios, groups of three.

335 *before*: in front of. It is possible that this is a later insertion, drawing attention to some members of Shakespeare's company who had danced in the masque of satyrs in Ben Jonson's *Oberon*, performed at the court of King James in 1611.

335–6 *not the . . . but*: even the worst of the trios can.

336 *square*: joiner's ruler.

340 *father*: A term of respect for an older man; Polixenes and the Shepherd have been in conversation throughout the 'satyr' dance, and Polixenes has succeeded in getting the information he wanted (see *4, 2, 45–49*).

344 *Sooth*: indeed.

345 *handed love*: carried on a love affair.
    was wont: was in the habit of, used to.

346 *she*: girl-friend.
    knacks: knick-knacks.

349 *nothing marted*: had no dealings.

350 *Interpretation . . . abuse*: should misinterpret.

351 *straited*: put in a tight corner.

352–3 *you make . . . her*: if you want to make sure you keep her happy.

355 *looks*: expects to receive.

356–7 *given . . . delivered*: Florizel distinguishes between the free gift of his heart and the formal, contractual, handing over of his love—which he attempts to do in lines 357–87.

357 *breathe my life*: utter vows that I shall keep all my life; the words are spoken to Perdita.

358 *ancient sir*: venerable gentleman—i.e. Polixenes.

360 *it*: i.e. the dove's down.

361 *Ethiopian*: At this time the word was used generally for any black person.
    bolted: sifted—a word usually describing flour.

362 *northern blasts*: The reference is to the icy winds blowing across the Caucasus mountains.

Servant
One three of them, by their own report, sir, hath
335 danced before the king; and not the worst of the
three but jumps twelve foot and a half by th'square.
Shepherd
Leave your prating. Since these good men are
pleased, let them come in; but quickly now.
Servant
Why, they stay at door, sir.

He lets in the herdsmen, who perform
their satyrs' dance and depart.

Polixenes
340 [*To* Shepherd] O, father, you'll know more of that
    hereafter.
[*To* Camillo] Is it not too far gone? 'Tis time to part
    them.
He's simple and tells much. [*To* Florizel] How now,
    fair shepherd!
Your heart is full of something that does take
Your mind from feasting. Sooth, when I was young
345 And handed love as you do, I was wont
To load my she with knacks. I would have ransack'd
The pedlar's silken treasury, and have pour'd it
To her acceptance: you have let him go
And nothing marted with him. If your lass
350 Interpretation should abuse and call this
Your lack of love or bounty, you were straited
For a reply, at least if you make a care
Of happy holding her.
Florizel
                        Old sir, I know
She prizes not such trifles as these are:
355 The gifts she looks from me are pack'd and lock'd
Up in my heart, which I have given already,
But not deliver'd. O, hear me breathe my life
Before this ancient sir, whom, it should seem,
Hath sometime lov'd! I take thy hand, this hand
360 As soft as dove's down and as white as it,
Or Ethiopian's tooth, or the fann'd snow that's
    bolted
By th'northern blasts twice o'er—

Polixenes

What follows this?
How prettily the young swain seems to wash
The hand was fair before! I have put you out.
365 But to your protestation: let me hear
What you profess.

Florizel

Do, and be witness to't.

Polixenes

And this my neighbour too?

Florizel

And he, and more
Than he, and men; the earth, the heavens, and all:
That were I crown'd the most imperial monarch,
370 Thereof most worthy, were I the fairest youth
That ever made eye swerve, had force and
knowledge
More than was ever man's, I would not prize them
Without her love; for her employ them all;
Commend them and condemn them to her service
375 Or to their own perdition.

Polixenes

Fairly offer'd.

Camillo

This shows a sound affection.

Shepherd

But, my daughter,
Say you the like to him?

Perdita

I cannot speak
So well, nothing so well; no, nor mean better.
By th'pattern of mine own thoughts I cut out
380 The purity of his.

Shepherd

Take hands, a bargain!
And, friends unknown, you shall bear witness to't.
I give my daughter to him, and will make
Her portion equal his.

Florizel

O, that must be
I'th'virtue of your daughter. One being dead,
385 I shall have more than you can dream of yet;

364 *was*: which was.

371 *force*: physical strength.

374–5 'Recommend all the good qualities to
her service and condemn all the bad
qualities to their own damnation'; a
similar grammatical structure is found
at *3, 2, 161–3*.

377 *like*: same.

379–80 Perdita, using the imagery of home-
dressmaking, understands that Florizel
must feel as she does.
380 *bargain*: For the Shepherd, the betrothal
handshake has the legality of a market
transaction.

383 *portion*: dowry.

384 *One being dead*: when a certain person is
dead.
385 *yet*: at present.

386 *Enough*: time enough.

388 *Soft*: go easy.

396 *altering rheums*: catarrhs that affect his
    mind.
397 *Dispute*: manage.

399 *being childish*: when he was a child.

403 *Something*: rather.
    Reason: it is reasonable that.

405 *all . . . else*: who delights in nothing else.

407 *yield*: admit.

409 *I not acquaint*: I am not telling.

Enough then for your wonder. But come on:
Contract us 'fore these witnesses.

Shepherd

                              Come, your hand;
And, daughter, yours.

Polixenes

                    Soft, swain, awhile, beseech you.
Have you a father?

Florizel

                    I have; but what of him?

Polixenes

390 Knows he of this?

Florizel

                    He neither does nor shall.

Polixenes

Methinks a father
Is at the nuptial of his son a guest
That best becomes the table. Pray you once more,
Is not your father grown incapable
395 Of reasonable affairs? Is he not stupid
With age and altering rheums? Can he speak? Hear?
Know man from man? Dispute his own estate?
Lies he not bed-rid? And again does nothing
But what he did being childish?

Florizel

                              No, good sir:
400 He has his health, and ampler strength indeed
Than most have of his age.

Polixenes

                         By my white beard,
You offer him, if this be so, a wrong
Something unfilial. Reason my son
Should choose himself a wife, but as good reason
405 The father, all whose joy is nothing else
But fair posterity, should hold some counsel
In such a business.

Florizel

                    I yield all this;
But for some other reasons, my grave sir,
Which 'tis not fit you know, I not acquaint
410 My father of this business.

Polixenes

                                    Let him know't.

Florizel

He shall not.

Polixenes

                          Prithee, let him.

Florizel

                                    No, he must not.

Shepherd

Let him, my son: he shall not need to grieve
At knowing of thy choice.

Florizel

                                    Come, come, he must not.

Mark our contract.

Polixenes

415 [*Removing his disguise*] Mark your divorce, young sir,
Whom son I dare not call: thou art too base
To be acknowledg'd. Thou a sceptre's heir,
That thus affects a sheep-hook?—Thou, old traitor,
I am sorry that by hanging thee I can
420 But shorten thy life one week.—And thou, fresh
      piece
Of excellent witchcraft, who of force must know
The royal fool thou cop'st with—

Shepherd

                                    O, my heart!

Polixenes

I'll have thy beauty scratch'd with briers and made
More homely than thy state.—For thee, fond boy,
425 If I may ever know thou dost but sigh
That thou no more shalt see this knack—as never
I mean thou shalt—we'll bar thee from succession;
Not hold thee of our blood, no, not our kin,
Far than Deucalion off. Mark thou my words!
430 Follow us to the court.—Thou, churl, for this time,
Though full of our displeasure, yet we free thee
From the dead blow of it.—And you, enchantment,
Worthy enough a herdsman—yea, him too,
That makes himself, but for our honour therein,
435 Unworthy thee—if ever henceforth thou
These rural latches to his entrance open,
Or hoop his body more with thy embraces,

414 *contract*: The betrothal contract could
      be as binding, morally and legally, as
      the marriage contract, although it was
      not recognized by the Church.
418 *affects*: is attracted to, loves.
      sheep-hook: shepherd's crook.

420-1 *fresh . . . witchcraft*: cunning young
      witch.
421 *of force*: of course.
422 *cop'st with*: are playing about with.
424 *homely*: plain, ordinary.
      fond: foolish.
426 *knack*: bit of a thing.
428 *hold . . . blood*: consider you to be
      related to me.
428-9 *not . . . off*: Polixenes is in effect
      saying 'I won't know you from Adam'.
      Deucalion, the Greek equivalent of
      Noah, re-established the human race
      after the flood.
430 *churl*: villain, peasant; the address is to
      the Shepherd.
432 *dead blow*: full force that would strike
      you dead.
      enchantment: Polixenes seems to
      appreciate Perdita's beauty even whilst
      condemning it as witchcraft.
433-5 *him too . . . thee*: Perdita would be
      worthy of Florizel—if it were not for his
      noble descent—although *he* has lowered
      himself to become unworthy of *her*.
436 *rural latches*: cottage doors—but
      Polixenes may be speaking
      metaphorically.

I will devise a death as cruel for thee
As thou art tender to't.   [*Exit*

Perdita

                                    Even here undone!
440 I was not much afeard; for once or twice
I was about to speak and tell him plainly,
The selfsame sun that shines upon his court
Hides not his visage from our cottage, but
Looks on alike. [*To* Florizel] Will't please you, sir,
     be gone?
445 I told you what would come of this. Beseech you,
Of your own state take care. This dream of mine—
Being now awake, I'll queen it no inch farther,
But milk my ewes, and weep.

Camillo

                                    Why, how now, father!
Speak ere thou die'st.

Shepherd

                                    I cannot speak nor think,
450 Nor dare to know that which I know. [*To* Florizel]
     O sir!
You have undone a man of fourscore three,
That thought to fill his grave in quiet, yea,
To die upon the bed my father died,
To lie close by his honest bones; but now
455 Some hangman must put on my shroud and lay me
Where no priest shovels in dust. [*To* Perdita] O
     cursed wretch,
That knew'st this was the prince and wouldst
     adventure
To mingle faith with him! Undone, undone!
If I might die within this hour, I have liv'd
460 To die when I desire.

                                                        [*Exit*

Florizel

                                    Why look you so upon me?
I am but sorry, not afeard; delay'd,
But nothing alter'd: what I was I am;
More straining on for plucking back, not following
My leash unwillingly.

Camillo

                                    Gracious my lord,
465 You know your father's temper. At this time

446   *state*: position.

447   *queen it*: stop behaving like a queen (at the sheepshearing feast), *and* forget all thoughts of being your queen.

449   *ere*: before; both Camillo and the Shepherd appear to have forgotten that the death sentence of line 419 was revoked at line 431.

451   *undone*: ruined.

456   *Where . . . dust*: without proper Christian burial—i.e. at the foot of the gallows.
457   *adventure*: take a risk.
458   *mingle faith*: join in a pledge (of marriage).

463–4   *More . . . unwillingly*: I'm more eager than ever to get on with things now that I'm being restrained, and I'm not going to be dragged back against my will.

He will allow no speech—which I do guess
You do not purpose to him—and as hardly
Will he endure your sight as yet, I fear.
Then till the fury of his highness settle
470 Come not before him.

Florizel
                                    I not purpose it.
I think Camillo?

Camillo
                        Even he, my lord.

Perdita
How often have I told you 'twould be thus!
How often said my dignity would last
But till 'twere known!

Florizel
                        It cannot fail but by
475 The violation of my faith; and then
Let Nature crush the sides o'th'earth together
And mar the seeds within! Lift up thy looks.
From my succession wipe me, father, I
Am heir to my affection.

Camillo
                        Be advis'd.

Florizel
480 I am, and by my fancy. If my reason
Will thereto be obedient, I have reason;
If not, my senses, better pleas'd with madness,
Do bid it welcome.

Camillo
                        This is desperate, sir.

Florizel
So call it, but it does fulfil my vow:
485 I needs must think it honesty. Camillo,
Not for Bohemia, nor the pomp that may
Be thereat glean'd; for all the sun sees or
The close earth wombs or the profound seas hides
In unknown fathoms, will I break my oath
490 To this my fair belov'd. Therefore, I pray you,
As you've e'er been my father's honour'd friend,
When he shall miss me—as, in faith, I mean not
To see him any more—cast your good counsels
Upon his passion. Let myself and fortune
495 Tug for the time to come. This you may know,

469 *highness*: haughtiness.

471 *Camillo?*: Florizel recognizes the
courtier.

477 *the seeds*: the sources of all life.

479 *affection*: passionate love.
      be advis'd: take warning, be sensible.

480 *fancy*: emotions. Philosophy taught that
the emotions should be subject to
reason, but Florizel reverses the two.
481 *I have reason*: I shall keep sane.

484 *So . . . vow*: you may call my behaviour
desperate, but I'm only keeping my
promise.

488 *wombs*: holds within itself.

494-5 *Let myself . . . come*: let me fight it out
with fortune to see what's going to
happen.

496 *deliver*: report.

498 *opportune*: The stress is on the second
      syllable—oppórtune.
499 *rides fast by*: is anchored nearby.

501–2 *Shall nothing . . . reporting*: won't do
      you any good to know, or me to tell
      you.

And so deliver: I am put to sea
With her who here I cannot hold on shore;
And most opportune to our need I have
A vessel rides fast by, but not prepar'd
500 For this design. What course I mean to hold
Shall nothing benefit your knowledge, nor
Concern me the reporting.

Camillo
                              O my lord,
I would your spirit were easier for advice,
Or stronger for your need.

503 *would*: wish.
      easier for: more open to.

Florizel
                              Hark, Perdita—
505 [*To* Camillo] I'll hear you by and by.

He draws Perdita *aside*

505–11 Camillo's lines, spoken 'aside' to the
      audience, point the direction for the
      play's final movement.

Camillo
                              He's irremovable,
Resolv'd for flight. Now were I happy if
His going I could frame to serve my turn,
Save him from danger, do him love and honour,

505 *irremovable*: immovable.

Purchase the sight again of dear Sicilia
510 And that unhappy king, my master, whom
I so much thirst to see.

Florizel
                                    Now, good Camillo,
I am so fraught with curious business that
I leave out ceremony.

Camillo
                        Sir, I think
You have heard of my poor services i'th'love
515 That I have borne your father?

Florizel
                                    Very nobly
Have you deserv'd: it is my father's music
To speak your deeds, not little of his care
To have them recompens'd as thought on.

Camillo
                                Well, my lord,
If you may please to think I love the king,
520 And through him what's nearest to him, which is
Your gracious self, embrace but my direction.
If your more ponderous and settled project
May suffer alteration, on mine honour,
I'll point you where you shall have such receiving
525 As shall become your highness: where you may
Enjoy your mistress, from the whom, I see,
There's no disjunction to be made but by—
As heavens forfend!—your ruin; marry her;
And, with my best endeavours in your absence,
530 Your discontenting father strive to qualify,
And bring him up to liking.

Florizel
                            How, Camillo,
May this, almost a miracle, be done?
That I may call thee something more than man,
And after that trust to thee.

Camillo
                                Have you thought on
535 A place whereto you'll go?

Florizel
                                Not any yet:
But as th'unthought-on accident is guilty

512 *fraught*: weighed down.
    curious: worrying, requiring care.

518 *as thought on*: as soon as they are
    thought of.

522 *more ponderous*: weightier, of greater
    importance (than Camillo's own plans).
    settled: fixed, finally decided on.
524–5 *you shall . . . highness*: you will be
    given a reception suitable for someone
    of your high rank.
527 *disjunction*: separation.
528 *forfend*: forbid.
529–31 *And, with . . . liking*: and when you
    are away from here I will make every
    endeavour both to pacify your father's
    anger and to bring him round to look
    favourably on you.

534 *after that*: accordingly.

536–7 *But as . . . wildly do*: since an
    unexpected mischance (i.e. their
    discovery by Polixenes) is provoking us
    to such unpremeditated action.

To what we wildly do, so we profess
Ourselves to be the slaves of chance, and flies
Of every wind that blows.

Camillo

                           Then list to me.
540 This follows, if you will not change your purpose
But undergo this flight: make for Sicilia,
And there present yourself and your fair princess—
For so I see she must be—'fore Leontes.
She shall be habited as it becomes
545 The partner of your bed. Methinks I see
Leontes opening his free arms and weeping
His welcomes forth; and asks the son forgiveness,
As 'twere i'th'father's person; kisses the hands
Of your fresh princess; o'er and o'er divides him
550 'Twixt his unkindness and his kindness: th'one
He chides to hell and bids the other grow
Faster than thought or time.

Florizel

                          Worthy Camillo,
What colour for my visitation shall I
Hold up before him?

Camillo

                        Sent by the king your father
555 To greet him and to give him comforts. Sir,
The manner of your bearing towards him, with
What you, as from your father, shall deliver—
Things known betwixt us three—I'll write you down,
The which shall point you forth at every sitting
560 What you must say: that he shall not perceive
But that you have your father's bosom there
And speak his very heart.

546 *opening . . . arms*: opening his arms freely.

548 *As 'twere . . . person*: as though you were your father.

549 *fresh*: young and lovely.

549–50 *o'er . . . kindness*: Camillo envisages Leontes torn between repentance for his unnatural behaviour to Polixenes and his natural affection for Polixenes' son.

553 *colour*: pretext, explanation.

555 *comforts*: assurances of friendship.

556 *The manner . . . bearing*: how you are to behave.

557 *as from*: as though it (the message) were from.

559 *sitting*: meeting.

561 *bosom*: personal confidence.

563 *sap*: meaning, life, sense.

564 *wild dedication*: abandoning.
565 *unpath'd*: uncharted.

567 *one*: i.e. one misery.

569 *stay*: hold.

571 *the . . . love*: what keeps love together.

573 *alters*: changes for the worse.

575 *take in*: overcome.

576 *these seven years*: for a very long time.

578–9 *as forward . . . birth*: she is as much superior to her upbringing as she is inferior to me in birth.
579 *our*: Florizel speaks in the 'royal plural'.

582 *blush you thanks*: Perdita, blushing, thanks Camillo for his compliments.
583 *the thorns we stand upon*: what a mess we're in; Florizel uses a proverbial expression.
585 *medicine*: physician.
586 *furnish'd . . . son*: equipped in a style befitting the son of the king of Bohemia.
587 *appear*: appear as such.

Florizel
                           I am bound to you.
There is some sap in this.
Camillo
                        A course more promising
Than a wild dedication of yourselves
565 To unpath'd waters, undream'd shores, most certain
To miseries enough: no hope to help you,
But as you shake off one to take another;
Nothing so certain as your anchors, who
Do their best office if they can but stay you
570 Where you'll be loath to be. Besides, you know
Prosperity's the very bond of love,
Whose fresh complexion and whose heart together
Affliction alters.
Perdita
                    One of these is true:
I think affliction may subdue the cheek,
575 But not take in the mind.
Camillo
                        Yea? Say you so?
There shall not at your father's house these seven years
Be born another such.
Florizel
                  My good Camillo,
She is as forward of her breeding as
She is i'th'rear' our birth.
Camillo
                  I cannot say 'tis pity
580 She lacks instructions, for she seems a mistress
To most that teach.
Perdita
                Your pardon, sir; for this
I'll blush you thanks.
Florizel
               My prettiest Perdita!
But O, the thorns we stand upon! Camillo—
Preserver of my father, now of me,
585 The medicine of our house—how shall we do?
We are not furnish'd like Bohemia's son,
Nor shall appear in Sicilia.

588 *fortunes*: possessions, estate.

591 *scene*: stage performance.

596 *table-book*: notebook, notepad.

597 *horn-ring*: ring made of horn (thought to be magic).

598 *fasting*: being quite empty.

601 *best in picture*: most suitable for picking—i.e. *both* easily accessible *and* worth stealing.

604 *pettitoes*: little pigs' trotters—i.e. his feet.

606-7 *stuck in ears*: were lost in their ears (compare line 188).

607 *placket*: petticoat-pocket (compare line 242).

608 *geld . . . purse*: cut off a purse from some man's codpiece (= the bag—'cod'—holding the penis—'piece').

610 *my sir's*: i.e. the Clown's.
admiring: wondering at.
nothing: triviality.

611 *picked and cut*: Autolycus operates as both pick-pocket and cut-purse.

612 *festival purses*: loaded purses brought to the feast.

614 *choughs*: jackdaws—birds attracted to bright objects.
chaff: junk, rubbish.

Camillo

          My lord,
Fear none of this. I think you know my fortunes
Do all lie there. It shall be so my care
590 To have you royally appointed as if
The scene you play were mine. For instance, sir,
That you may know you shall not want, one word.

They talk aside

Enter Autolycus

Autolycus

Ha, ha, what a fool Honesty is! And Trust, his sworn
brother, a very simple gentleman! I have sold all my
595 trumpery: not a counterfeit stone, not a ribbon, glass,
pomander, brooch, table-book, ballad, knife, tape,
glove, shoe-tie, bracelet, horn-ring, to keep my pack
from fasting. They throng who should buy first, as if
my trinkets had been hallowed and brought a
600 benediction to the buyer; by which means I saw whose
purse was best in picture; and what I saw, to my good
use I remembered. My clown, who wants but
something to be a reasonable man, grew so in love with
the wenches' song that he would not stir his pettitoes
605 till he had both tune and words; which so drew the rest
of the herd to me that all their other senses stuck in
ears: you might have pinched a placket, it was senseless;
'twas nothing to geld a codpiece of a purse; I would
have filed keys off that hung in chains. No hearing, no
610 feeling, but my sir's song, and admiring the nothing of
it. So that in this time of lethargy I picked and cut most
of their festival purses; and had not the old man come
in with a hubbub against his daughter and the king's
son and scared my choughs from the chaff, I had not
615 left a purse alive in the whole army.

Camillo, Florizel, *and* Perdita *come forward*

Camillo

Nay, but my letters, by this means being there
So soon as you arrive, shall clear that doubt.

    Florizel

And those that you'll procure from King Leontes—

Camillo
Shall satisfy your father.

Perdita
                                Happy be you!
620 All that you speak shows fair.

Camillo
[*Seeing* Autolycus]   Who have we here?
We'll make an instrument of this, omit
Nothing may give us aid.

Autolycus
[*Aside*] If they have overheard me now—why,
hanging!

Camillo
625 How now, good fellow! Why shak'st thou so?
Fear not, man: here's no harm intended to thee.

Autolycus
I am a poor fellow, sir.

Camillo
Why, be so still: here's nobody will steal that
from thee. Yet for the outside of thy poverty we
630 must make an exchange; therefore discase thee
instantly—thou must think there's a necessity in't—
and change garments with this gentleman. Though
the pennyworth on his side be the worst, yet hold
thee, there's some boot.

He gives him money

Autolycus
635 I am a poor fellow, sir. [*Aside*] I know ye well
enough.

Camillo
Nay, prithee, dispatch. The gentleman is half flayed
already.

619 *Happy be you*: bless you.
620 *shows fair*: sounds good.

621 *this*: this fellow.

624 *hanging*: it will mean hanging; thieves could be hanged for the theft of items more than 12 pence in value.

630 *discase thee*: take your clothes off.
631 *think*: understand.

633 *pennyworth*: i.e. bargain.
633-4 *yet hold thee*: just wait a minute.
634 *boot*: compensation.

637 *flayed*: skinned, stripped.

639   *in earnest*: serious.
639–40   *I smell . . . on't*: I can see what they are up to.

641   *Dispatch*: get on with it, hurry.

642   *earnest*: something to be going on with, part-payment in advance—with a play on the *earnest* of line 639.

645–6   *let . . . to ye*: and I hope I shall be proved right in calling you so.

647   *covert*: hiding place.

648   *pluck it*: pull it down.
649   *Dismantle you*: take off these robes you are wearing (as queen of the feast). *disliken*: disguise.
650   *truth of your own seeming*: your real appearance.
651   *eyes over*: spies watching everything (for the king).
652   *undescried*: undetected.

657   *forgot*: This is nothing more than a device to allow for Camillo's explanation to the audience.

Autolycus
Are you in earnest, sir? [*Aside*] I smell the trick
640 on't.
Florizel
Dispatch, I prithee.
Autolycus
Indeed, I have had earnest, but I cannot with conscience take it.
Camillo
Unbuckle, unbuckle.

Florizel and Autolycus *exchange garments*

645 Fortunate mistress—let my prophecy
Come home to ye!—you must retire yourself
Into some covert; take your sweetheart's hat
And pluck it o'er your brows, muffle your face,
Dismantle you, and, as you can, disliken
650 The truth of your own seeming, that you may—
For I do fear eyes over—to shipboard
Get undescried.
Perdita
                    I see the play so lies
That I must bear a part.
Camillo
                              No remedy.
Have you done there?
Florizel
                         Should I now meet my father,
655 He would not call me son.
Camillo
                              Nay, you shall have no hat.

He gives the hat to Perdita

Come, lady, come. Farewell, my friend.
Autolycus
                                          Adieu, sir.
Florizel
O Perdita, what have we twain forgot!
Pray you, a word.
Camillo
[*Aside*] What I do next shall be to tell the king

660 Of this escape and whither they are bound;
Wherein my hope is I shall so prevail
To force him after: in whose company
I shall re-view Sicilia, for whose sight
I have a woman's longing.
    Florizel
                        Fortune speed us!
665 Thus we set on, Camillo, to th'seaside.
    Camillo
The swifter speed the better.
            [*Exeunt* Florizel, Perdita, *and* Camillo
    Autolycus
I understand the business, I hear it. To have an open
ear, a quick eye, and a nimble hand is necessary for
a cutpurse; a good nose is requisite also, to smell out
670 work for th'other senses. I see this is the time that the
unjust man doth thrive. What an exchange had this
been without boot! What a boot is here, with this
exchange! Sure, the gods do this year connive at us,
and we may do anything extempore. The prince
675 himself is about a piece of iniquity—stealing away
from his father, with his clog at his heels. If I thought
it were a piece of honesty to acquaint the king withal,
I would not do't. I hold it the more knavery to conceal
it; and therein am I constant to my profession.

            Enter Clown *and* Shepherd

680 Aside, aside! Here is more matter for a hot brain.
Every lane's end, every shop, church, session,
hanging, yields a careful man work.
    Clown
See, see, what a man you are now! There is no other
way but to tell the king she's a changeling and none
685 of your flesh and blood.
    Shepherd
Nay, but hear me.
    Clown
Nay, but hear me.
    Shepherd
Go to, then.
    Clown
She being none of your flesh and blood, your flesh

690 and blood has not offended the king; and so your
flesh and blood is not to be punished by him. Show
those things you found about her, those secret
things, all but what she has with her. This being
done, let the law go whistle, I warrant you.

Shepherd

695 I will tell the king all, every word—yea, and his son's
pranks too; who, I may say, is no honest man,
neither to his father nor to me, to go about to make
me the king's brother-in-law.

Clown

Indeed, brother-in-law was the farthest off you could
700 have been to him; and then your blood had been the
dearer by I know not how much an ounce.

Autolycus

[*Aside*] Very wisely, puppies!

Shepherd

Well, let us to the king. There is that in this fardel
will make him scratch his beard.

Autolycus

705 [*Aside*] I know not what impediment this complaint
may be to the flight of my master.

Clown

Pray heartily he be at palace.

Autolycus

[*Aside*] Though I am not naturally honest, I am so
sometimes by chance. Let me pocket up my pedlar's
710 excrement.

He takes off his false beard

How now, rustics! Whither are you bound?

Shepherd

To th'palace, an it like your worship.

Autolycus

Your affairs there, what, with whom, the condition of
that fardel, the place of your dwelling, your names,
715 your ages, of what having, breeding, and anything
that is fitting to be known, discover.

Clown

We are but plain fellows, sir.

Autolycus

A lie: you are rough and hairy. Let me have no lying:
it becomes none but tradesmen, and they often give

694 *go whistle*: hang itself (a proverbial
expression).

703 *fardel*: bundle.
704 *scratch his beard*: i.e. think hard.
705 *my master*: Autolycus has already told us
that he had been servant to Florizel (4,
3, 13; 4, 4, 635).

710 *excrement*: facial hair.

712 *an it like*: if it please.
713 *affairs*: business.
condition: nature.

715 *having*: property.
breeding: upbringing.
716 *discover*: disclose.

720 *give . . . the lie*: cheat us soldiers (by giving short measure or poor quality).
721 *stamped coin*: current money.
   stabbing steel: drawn sword—the soldier's usual retort.
722 *give*: i.e. because it is paid for.
723–4 'You would probably have told us a lie, sir, if you had not seen your mistake and corrected yourself' ('they often give . . . we pay them . . . therefore they do not give . . .').
724 *with the manner*: in the act of.
725 *an't like you*: if it please you, if I might ask.
727 *enfoldings*: i.e. the clothing received from Florizel.
728 *measure*: movement (as in a formal dance).
729–30 *Reflect . . . contempt*: do I not look down on your humble status with the contempt of the court.
730–1 *for that . . . business*: just because I am trying to insinuate myself into your confidence in order to ferret out your business.
732 *cap-à-pie*: cap-à-pied, from head to foot.

739 *pheasant*: The Clown knows only the courts of local justices—where bribery with gifts of poultry was common practice.
742–4 Speaking in a parody of court language, Autolycus falls into blank verse—also rhyming the Shepherd's 'hen' with 'men'.
745 *be but*: be anything but.

720 us soldiers the lie; but we pay them for it with stamped coin, not stabbing steel; therefore they do not give us the lie.

Clown
Your worship had like to have given us one, if you had not taken yourself with the manner.

Shepherd
725 Are you a courtier, an't like you, sir?

Autolycus
Whether it like me or no, I am a courtier. Seest thou not the air of the court in these enfoldings? Hath not my gait in it the measure of the court? Receives not thy nose court-odour from me? Reflect I not on thy
730 baseness court-contempt? Think'st thou, for that I insinuate, to toaze from thee thy business, I am therefore no courtier? I am courtier cap-à-pie; and one that will either push on or pluck back thy business there; whereupon I command thee to open
735 thy affair.

Shepherd
My business, sir, is to the king.

Autolycus
What advocate hast thou to him?

Shepherd
I know not, an't like you.

Clown
Advocate's the court-word for a pheasant: say you
740 have none.

Shepherd
None, sir; I have no pheasant, cock nor hen.

Autolycus
How blessed are we that are not simple men!
Yet Nature might have made me as these are:
Therefore I'll not disdain.

Clown
745 [*Aside to* Shepherd] This cannot be but a great courtier.

Shepherd
His garments are rich, but he wears them not handsomely.

Clown
He seems to be the more noble in being fantastical.

747 *garments*: It was by common stage
    convention that the Shepherd should
    not recognize the clothing as that worn
    by Florizel—and Shakespeare seems to
    have forgotten that Florizel was dressed
    in 'swain's wearing' (line 9).
748 *handsomely*: elegantly.
749 *fantastical*: peculiar in his behaviour.
750–1 *picking on's teeth*: Autolycus would be
    using a toothpick, once the sign affected
    by travellers—and probably unfamiliar
    to the rustics.
754 *this fardel and box*: Presumably the
    clothes worn by the baby are rolled up
    in the 'fardel', whilst the 'box' contains
    the remainder of the gold and also the
    scroll left by Antigonus.

762 *capable*: capable of understanding.
766 *in handfast*: under arrest.

770 *wit*: ingenuity.
771 *germane*: related.

775 *offer*: attempt, scheme.
776 *grace*: the nobility.

750 A great man, I'll warrant. I know by the picking on's teeth.

Autolycus

The fardel there, what's i'th'fardel? Wherefore that box?

Shepherd

Sir, there lies such secrets in this fardel and box, 755 which none must know but the king; and which he shall know within this hour, if I may come to th'speech of him.

Autolycus

Age, thou hast lost thy labour.

Shepherd

Why, sir?

Autolycus

760 The king is not at the palace; he is gone aboard a new ship, to purge melancholy and air himself: for, if thou be'st capable of things serious, thou must know the king is full of grief.

Shepherd

So 'tis said, sir: about his son, that should have 765 married a shepherd's daughter.

Autolycus

If that shepherd be not in handfast, let him fly: the curses he shall have, the tortures he shall feel, will break the back of man, the heart of monster.

Clown

Think you so, sir?

Autolycus

770 Not he alone shall suffer what wit can make heavy and vengeance bitter; but those that are germane to him, though removed fifty times, shall all come under the hangman—which, though it be great pity, yet it is necessary. An old sheep-whistling rogue, a 775 ram-tender, to offer to have his daughter come into grace? Some say he shall be stoned; but that death is too soft for him, say I. Draw our throne into a sheep-cote? All deaths are too few, the sharpest too easy.

Clown

Has the old man e'er a son, sir, do you hear, an't like 780 you, sir?

781–9 *shall be . . . blown to death*:
Shakespeare and his audience could
have read about such tortures in the
works of Boccaccio, or heard reports of
the atrocities inflicted by the Spanish in
America.

783 *and a dram*: and a little bit more.
784–5 *hot infusion*: stimulant.
786 *prognostication*: the weather forecast for
the year.
788 *where he*: i.e. the sun.

792–3 *Being . . . considered*: for a small
consideration.
793 *where he is aboard*: Autolycus is already
formulating a plan: 'he' refers to the
prince, and not—as the rustics think—
to the king.
794 *tender*: escort.

797 *Close*: make a bargain.
798 *and though*: even though.
799 *led by the nose*: i.e. easily led, like a
captive bear.

803 *that gold*: all of the gold that.

808 *moiety*: portion, half-share.

810 *case*: condition *and* skin.

Autolycus

He has a son: who shall be flayed alive; then, 'nointed
over with honey, set on the head of a wasp's nest; then
stand till he be three-quarters and a dram dead; then
recovered again with aqua-vitae or some other hot
785 infusion; then, raw as he is, and in the hottest day
prognostication proclaims, shall he be set against a
brick wall, the sun looking with a southward eye upon
him, where he is to behold him with flies blown to
death. But what talk we of these traitorly rascals,
790 whose miseries are to be smiled at, their offences being
so capital? Tell me, for you seem to be honest, plain
men, what you have to the king. Being something
gently considered, I'll bring you where he is aboard,
tender your persons to his presence, whisper him in
795 your behalfs; and if it be in man besides the king to
effect your suits, here is man shall do it.

Clown

He seems to be of great authority. Close with him,
give him gold; and though authority be a stubborn
bear, yet he is oft led by the nose with gold. Show the
800 inside of your purse to the outside of his hand, and
no more ado. Remember, stoned, and flayed alive!

Shepherd

An't please you, sir, to undertake the business for
us, here is that gold I have. I'll make it as much
more, and leave this young man in pawn till I bring
805 it you.

Autolycus

After I have done what I promised?

Shepherd

Ay, sir.

Autolycus

Well, give me the moiety.
[*To the* Clown] Are you a party in this business?

Clown

810 In some sort, sir: but though my case be a pitiful
one, I hope I shall not be flayed out of it.

Autolycus

O, that's the case of the shepherd's son. Hang him,
he'll be made an example.

Clown

[*Aside to* Shepherd] Comfort, good comfort! We must

815 to the king and show our strange sights. He must know
'tis none of your daughter, nor my sister; we are gone
else. [*To* Autolycus] Sir, I will give you as much as this
old man does, when the business is performed; and
remain, as he says, your pawn till it be brought you.

Autolycus

820 I will trust you. Walk before toward the seaside; go
on the right hand: I will but look upon the hedge,
and follow you.

816–17 *gone else*: ruined otherwise.
821 *look . . . hedge*: Pretending he wants to
relieve himself, Autolycus allows the
Shepherd and the Clown to leave the
stage without him, so that he can
address the audience.

Clown

[*Aside to* Shepherd] We are blest in this man, as I
may say, even blest.

Shepherd

825 Let's before, as he bids us. He was provided to do us
good.

[*Exeunt* Shepherd *and* Clown

Autolycus

If I had a mind to be honest, I see Fortune would not
suffer me: she drops booties in my mouth. I am
courted now with a double occasion: gold, and a
830 means to do the prince my master good; which who
knows how that may turn back to my advancement?
I will bring these two moles, these blind ones, aboard
him. If he think it fit to shore them again, and that
the complaint they have to the king concerns him
835 nothing, let him call me rogue for being so far
officious; for I am proof against that title, and what
shame else belongs to't. To him will I present them:
there may be matter in it.

[*Exit*

828 *booties*: rewards, prizes.
829 *occasion*: opportunity.

831 *turn back*: rebound, turn out.
832–3 *aboard him*: on to his (the prince's)
ship.
833 *shore them*: put them ashore.

836 *proof against*: immune to.
836–7 *what shame else*: whatever other
disgrace.
838 *there . . . in it*: I might get something for
myself out of his.

Act 5

Act 5   Scene 1

Leaving the Bohemian characters to find
their own way out of trouble, the audience is
returned to Sicilia where Leontes is still
grieving over the events of sixteen years ago.
His reverie is interrupted by the surprise
arrival of Florizel and Perdita, but their
welcome is short-lived. The angry Polixenes
is in hot pursuit.

2 *sorrow*: penance.

6 *them*: i.e. your sins.

8 *blemishes in them*: wrongs done to them;
   or faults in comparison with these.

Scene 1

Enter Leontes, Cleomenes, Dion, Paulina,
and others

Cleomenes
Sir, you have done enough, and have perform'd
A saint-like sorrow. No fault could you make
Which you have not redeem'd; indeed, paid down
More penitence than done trespass. At the last,
5 Do as the heavens have done, forget your evil;
With them forgive yourself.

Leontes
                                    Whilst I remember
Her and her virtues, I cannot forget
My blemishes in them, and so still think of
The wrong I did myself: which was so much
10 That heirless it hath made my kingdom and
Destroy'd the sweet'st companion that e'er man
Bred his hopes out of.

Paulina
                                 True, too true, my lord.
If one by one you wedded all the world,
Or from the all that are took something good
15 To make a perfect woman, she you kill'd
Would be unparallel'd.

Leontes
                                 I think so. Kill'd!
She I kill'd! I did so; but thou strik'st me
Sorely to say I did. It is as bitter
Upon thy tongue as in my thought. Now, good now,
20 Say so but seldom.

Cleomenes
                           Not at all, good lady.

You might have spoken a thousand things that would
Have done the time more benefit and grac'd
Your kindness better.

Paulina
                                    You are one of those
Would have him wed again.

Dion
                                    If you would not so,
25 You pity not the state, nor the remembrance
Of his most sovereign name; consider little
What dangers by his highness' fail of issue
May drop upon his kingdom and devour
Incertain lookers-on. What were more holy
30 Than to rejoice the former queen is well?
What holier than, for royalty's repair,
For present comfort and for future good,
To bless the bed of majesty again
With a sweet fellow to't?

Paulina
                                    There is none worthy,
35 Respecting her that's gone. Besides the gods
Will have fulfill'd their secret purposes:
For has not the divine Apollo said,
Is't not the tenor of his oracle,
That King Leontes shall not have an heir
40 Till his lost child be found? Which that it shall
Is all as monstrous to our human reason
As my Antigonus to break his grave
And come again to me; who, on my life,
Did perish with the infant. 'Tis your counsel
45 My lord should to the heavens be contrary,
Oppose against their wills. [*To* Leontes] Care not
      for issue.
The crown will find an heir. Great Alexander
Left his to th'worthiest; so his successor
Was like to be the best.

Leontes
                                    Good Paulina,
50 Who hast the memory of Hermione,
I know, in honour, O that ever I
Had squar'd me to thy counsel! Then even now
I might have look'd upon my queen's full eyes,
Have taken treasure from her lips—

25–6 *You pity . . . name*: you have no pity for the state, nor any thought for the perpetuation of the royal name.

26 *consider little*: you must give a little thought to.

27 *fail of issue*: want of an heir.

29 *Incertain lookers-on*: those who stand by not knowing what to do.

30 *is well*: is at rest (in her grave).

35 *Respecting*: in comparison with.

36 'Insist on having their secret plans carried out.'

38 *tenor*: message, subject-matter.

42 *As*: as it would be for.

45 *contrary*: The stress is on the second syllable.

47 *Alexander*: Alexander the Great, king of Macedonia in the third century BC, who was held to be a model for all conquerors and kings.

51–2 *that ever . . . counsel*: if only I had always been ruled by your advice.

Paulina

And left them

55 More rich for what they yielded.

Leontes

Thou speak'st truth.

No more such wives, therefore no wife: one worse,
And better us'd, would make her sainted spirit
Again possess her corpse, and on this stage,
Where we offenders move, appear soul-vex'd,

60 And begin, 'Why to me?'

Paulina

Had she such power,

She had just cause.

Leontes

She had, and would incense me

To murder her I married.

Paulina

I should so.

Were I the ghost that walk'd, I'd bid you mark
Her eye, and tell me for what dull part in't

65 You chose her; then I'd shriek, that even your ears
Should rift to hear me; and the words that follow'd
Should be 'Remember mine.'

Leontes

Stars, stars,

And all eyes else dead coals! Fear thou no wife;
I'll have no wife, Paulina.

Paulina

Will you swear

70 Never to marry but by my free leave?

Leontes

Never, Paulina, so be blest my spirit!

Paulina

Then, good my lords, bear witness to his oath.

Cleomenes

You tempt him over-much.

Paulina

Unless another,

As like Hermione as is her picture,

75 Affront his eye.

Cleomenes

Good madam—

---

56 *No more*: there are no more.

59 *soul-vex'd*: perplexed in her soul.
60 *Why to me*: why have you done this to me.

61 *incense*: provoke.

62 *I should so*: this is what I would do.

65 *even your ears*: your very ears.
66 *rift*: burst, be split.
67 *mine*: i.e. my eyes.

70 *free*: unforced, willing.

75 *Affront*: confront, come before.

Paulina
                                        I have done.
Yet if my lord will marry—if you will, sir,
No remedy, but you will—give me the office
To choose you a queen: she shall not be so young
As was your former, but she shall be such
80 As, walk'd your first queen's ghost, it should take joy
To see her in your arms.
Leontes
                              My true Paulina,
We shall not marry till thou bid'st us.
Paulina
                                            That
Shall be when your first queen's again in breath;
Never till then.

Enter a Gentleman

Gentleman
85 One that gives out himself Prince Florizel
Son of Polixenes, with his princess—she
The fairest I have yet beheld—desires access
To your high presence.
Leontes
                              What with him? He comes not
Like to his father's greatness. His approach
90 So out of circumstance and sudden tells us
'Tis not a visitation fram'd, but forc'd
By need and accident. What train?
Gentleman
                                        But few,
And those but mean.
Leontes
                              His princess, say you, with him?
Gentleman
Ay, the most peerless piece of earth, I think,
95 That e'er the sun shone bright on.
Paulina
                                        O Hermione,
As every present time doth boast itself
Above a better gone, so must thy grave
Give way to what's seen now. [*To the* Gentleman]
    Sir, you yourself
Have said and writ so—but your writing now

80 *walk'd . . . ghost*: if Hermione's ghost were to walk.

83 *in breath*: alive.

85 *gives out*: proclaims, announces.

88 *What with him*: what company is with him.
89 *Like to*: in a manner appropriate to.
90 *out of circumstance*: without ceremony. *sudden*: unexpected.
91 *fram'd*: planned, organized.
92 *train*: entourage.
93 *mean*: shabby.

97 *so must thy grave*: so must you, now that you are in your grave.

99 *writ*: written.

100 *colder than that theme*: more dead than
its subject (Hermione).

102 *shrewdly*: quickly, sharply.

107 *begin a sect*: start a new religious belief.

108 *professors*: religious believers.
proselytes: converts, followers.

109 *Not women*: surely this doesn't include
women.

113 *assisted with*: accompanied by.

116 *pair'd*: matched.

122 *Unfurnish . . . reason*: send me out of
my mind.

124 *print . . . off*: make a perfect copy of
your father.

100 Is colder than that theme—she had not been,
Nor was not to be, equall'd; thus your verse
Flow'd with her beauty once. 'Tis shrewdly ebb'd
To say you have seen a better.

Gentleman

Pardon, madam.
The one I have almost forgot—your pardon;
105 The other, when she has obtain'd your eye
Will have your tongue too. This is a creature,
Would she begin a sect, might quench the zeal
Of all professors else, make proselytes
Of who she but bid follow.

Paulina

How? Not women!

Gentleman
110 Women will love her that she is a woman
More worth than any man; men that she is
The rarest of all women.

Leontes

Go, Cleomenes:
Yourself, assisted with your honour'd friends,
Bring them to our embracement.

[*Exeunt* Cleomenes *and others*
Still, 'tis strange
115 He thus should steal upon us.

Paulina

Had our prince,
Jewel of children, seen this hour, he had pair'd
Well with this lord: there was not full a month
Between their births.

Leontes

Prithee, no more! Cease! Thou
know'st
He dies to me again when talk'd of. Sure,
120 When I shall see this gentleman thy speeches
Will bring me to consider that which may
Unfurnish me of reason. They are come.

Enter Florizel, Perdita, Cleomenes, *and
others*

Your mother was most true to wedlock, prince:
For she did print your royal father off,

126 *hit*: copied.

135 *Amity*: friendship.
135-7 *whom . . . on him*: to see him once
   more is what makes me want to go on
   living, although my life is a misery to
   me.

139 *at friend*: in friendship.
140 *but*: but that, if it were not for.
141 *Which . . . times*: which comes with old
   age.
141-2 *hath something . . . ability*: has taken
   away some of the strength he would like
   to have.
144 *Measur'd*: crossed the length of.

148 *offices*: official friendly greetings.
149 *rarely kind*: wonderfully kind (= friendly
   and brotherly).
149-50 *as interpreters . . . slackness*: make it
   plain to me that I have been most
   remiss (in not sending similar greetings
   to Polixenes).
153 *Neptune*: god of the sea.
154 *pains*: trouble.
155 *adventure*: risk.

156 *Libya . . . Smalus*: A background has
   been invented for Perdita! Shakespeare
   draws on Plutarch's *Life of Dion* which
   describes a voyage from Libya to a
   Sicilian village ruled by a Carthaginian
   captain called Synalus—see 'Leading
   Characters', p.vii.

125 Conceiving you. Were I but twenty-one,
   Your father's image is so hit in you,
   His very air, that I should call you brother,
   As I did him, and speak of something wildly
   By us perform'd before. Most dearly welcome,
130 And your fair princess—goddess! O! Alas,
   I lost a couple that 'twixt heaven and earth
   Might thus have stood, begetting wonder, as
   You, gracious couple, do. And then I lost—
   All mine own folly—the society,
135 Amity too, of your brave father, whom,
   Though bearing misery, I desire my life
   Once more to look on him.

Florizel
                              By his command
   Have I here touch'd Sicilia, and from him
   Give you all greetings that a king, at friend,
140 Can send his brother; and but infirmity,
   Which waits upon worn times, hath something seiz'd
   His wish'd ability, he had himself
   The lands and waters 'twixt your throne and his
   Measur'd to look upon you, whom he loves—
145 He bade me say so—more than all the sceptres
   And those that bear them living.

Leontes
                              O my brother—
   Good gentleman—the wrongs I have done thee stir
   Afresh within me; and these thy offices,
   So rarely kind, are as interpreters
150 Of my behindhand slackness!—Welcome hither
   As is the spring to th'earth! And hath he too
   Expos'd this paragon to th'fearful usage,
   At least ungentle, of the dreadful Neptune
   To greet a man not worth her pains, much less
155 Th'adventure of her person?

Florizel
                              Good my lord,
   She came from Libya.

Leontes
                              Where the warlike Smalus,
   That noble, honour'd lord, is fear'd and lov'd?

Florizel

Most royal sir, from thence; from him whose
        daughter
His tears proclaim'd his, parting with her; thence,
160 A prosperous south wind friendly, we have cross'd,
To execute the charge my father gave me
For visiting your highness. My best train
I have from your Sicilian shores dismiss'd;
Who for Bohemia bend, to signify
165 Not only my success in Libya, sir,
But my arrival, and my wife's, in safety
Here where we are.

Leontes

                    The blessed gods
Purge all infection from our air whilst you
Do climate here! You have a holy father,
170 A graceful gentleman, against whose person,
So sacred as it is, I have done sin:
For which the heavens, taking angry note,
Have left me issueless; and your father's bless'd,
As he from heaven merits it, with you,
175 Worthy his goodness. What might I have been,
Might I a son and daughter now have look'd on,
Such goodly things as you!

Enter a Lord

Lord

                                Most noble sir,
That which I shall report will bear no credit,
Were not the proof so nigh. Please you, great sir,
180 Bohemia greets you from himself by me;
Desires you to attach his son, who has—
His dignity and duty both cast off—
Fled from his father, from his hopes, and with
A shepherd's daughter.

Leontes

                        Where's Bohemia? Speak.

Lord

185 Here in your city: I now came from him.
I speak amazedly, and it becomes
My marvel and my message. To your court
Whiles he was hast'ning—in the chase, it seems,
Of this fair couple—meets he on the way

160 *friendly*: being favourable.

162 *my best train*: the better part of my
    entourage.

164 *bend*: are bound.

165 *success*: i.e. in winning the daughter of
    the 'warlike Smalus'.

169 *climate*: remain in our part of the world.
    holy: honourable.

170 *graceful*: full of [divine] grace, virtuous.

173 *and*: on the other hand.

179 *nigh*: near, certain.

180 *Bohemia*: the king of Bohemia,
    Polixenes.

181 *attach*: arrest.

182 *dignity and duty*: dignity as a prince and
    duty of a son.

186 *amazedly*: confusedly.
    becomes: is suitable for.

190 The father of this seeming lady, and
Her brother, having both their country quitted
With this young prince.

Florizel

Camillo has betray'd me;
Whose honour and whose honesty till now
Endur'd all weathers.

Lord

Lay't so to his charge.
195 He's with the king your father.

Leontes

Who? Camillo?

Lord

Camillo, sir; I spake with him; who now
Has these poor men in question. Never saw I
Wretches so quake: they kneel, they kiss the earth;
Forswear themselves as often as they speak;
200 Bohemia stops his ears, and threatens them
With divers deaths in death.

Perdita

O my poor father!
The heaven sets spies upon us, will not have
Our contract celebrated.

Leontes

You are married?

Florizel

We are not, sir, nor are we like to be.
205 The stars, I see, will kiss the valleys first:
The odds for high and low's alike.

Leontes

My lord,
Is this the daughter of a king?

Florizel

She is,
When once she is my wife.

Leontes

That 'once', I see by your good father's speed,
210 Will come on very slowly. I am sorry,
Most sorry, you have broken from his liking,
Where you were tied in duty; and as sorry
Your choice is not so rich in worth as beauty,
That you might well enjoy her.

194 *weathers*: troubles.
Lay't . . . charge: accuse him of it.

197 *Has . . . in question*: is interrogating
these poor fellows.

201 *divers deaths in death*: different ways of
torturing them to death.

202 *heaven*: immortal gods.
spies: informers.

206 'The chances are the same, whether
you're rich or poor.'

Florizel

Dear, look up.

215 Though Fortune, visible an enemy,
Should chase us, with my father, power no jot
Hath she to change our loves. Beseech you, sir,
Remember since you ow'd no more to Time
Than I do now. With thought of such affections
220 Step forth mine advocate: at your request
My father will grant precious things as trifles.

Leontes
Would he do so, I'd beg your precious mistress,
Which he counts but a trifle.

Paulina

Sir, my liege,
Your eye hath too much youth in't. Not a month
225 'Fore your queen died she was more worth such
gazes
Than what you look on now.

Leontes

I thought of her
Even in these looks I made. But your petition
Is yet unanswer'd. I will to your father.
Your honour not o'erthrown by your desires,
230 I am friend to them and you; upon which errand
I now go toward him. Therefore follow me,
And mark what way I make. Come, good my lord.

[*Exeunt*

Act 5   Scene 2

With Autolycus, we hear of the amazing
events that have happened off-stage. The
Gentlemen of Leontes' court were present at
a great scene of recognition, and the details
are recounted in excited prose before they
leave to witness the next wonder. The
Shepherd and his son, having been rewarded
for the parts they have played, rejoice at their
good fortune.

3 *fardel*: bundle.

---

215 *visible an enemy*: actually to be seen as
an enemy.

218–19 *Remember . . . I do now*: think of the
time when you were as young as I am
now.

222 *I'd beg*: i.e. for himself.

229 'If your emotions haven't overstepped
the bounds of honour.'

232 *way*: success.

Scene 2

Enter Autolycus *and a* Gentleman

Autolycus
Beseech you, sir, were you present at this
relation?

First Gentleman
I was by at the opening of the fardel, heard the old
shepherd deliver the manner how he found it;

5 *after*: when we had got over.

5 whereupon, after a little amazedness, we were all
commanded out of the chamber. Only this methought
I heard the shepherd say: he found the child.
Autolycus
I would most gladly know the issue of it.
First Gentleman
I make a broken delivery of the business; but the

9 *broken delivery*: disjointed account.

10 changes I perceived in the king and Camillo were very
notes of admiration. They seemed almost, with
staring on one another, to tear the cases of their eyes.

11 *notes of admiration*: exclamations of
wonderment.
12 *to tear . . . eyes*: i.e. their eyes were
almost starting out of their heads.

There was speech in their dumbness, language in
their very gesture. They looked as they had heard of a

15 *notable*: remarkable.

15 world ransomed, or one destroyed. A notable passion
of wonder appeared in them; but the wisest beholder
that knew no more but seeing could not say if

17 *seeing*: what he saw.
18 *importance*: import, meaning.
18–19 *in the . . . needs be*: it had to be an
extreme case of one or the other.

th'importance were joy or sorrow: but in the extremity
of the one it must needs be.

Enter another Gentleman

20 Here comes a gentleman that haply knows more.
The news, Rogero?
Second Gentleman
Nothing but bonfires. The oracle is fulfilled: the

22 *bonfires*: Most village festivities include
the lighting of celebratory bonfires.

24 *ballad-makers*: See note on *4, 4, 187*.

king's daughter is found. Such a deal of wonder is
broken out within this hour that ballad-makers
25 cannot be able to express it.

Enter a third Gentleman

Here comes the Lady Paulina's steward; he can deliver
you more. How goes it now, sir? This news, which is
called true, is so like an old tale that the verity of it
is in strong suspicion. Has the king found his heir?
Third Gentleman

30 *pregnant by circumstance*: made
convincing by circumstantial evidence.

32 *unity in the proofs*: consistency in the
evidence.

30 Most true, if ever truth were pregnant by circumstance.
That which you hear you'll swear you see, there is
such unity in the proofs: the mantle of Queen
Hermione's; her jewel about the neck of it; the letters
of Antigonus found with it, which they know to be his

35 *character*: handwriting.
36 *affection*: quality.
37 *breeding*: upbringing.

35 character; the majesty of the creature in resemblance of
the mother; the affection of nobleness which nature
shows above her breeding, and many other evidences
proclaim her with all certainty to be the king's
daughter. Did you see the meeting of the two kings?

Second Gentleman

40 No.

Third Gentleman

Then have you lost a sight which was to be seen,
cannot be spoken of. There might you have beheld
one joy crown another, so and in such manner that it
seemed sorrow wept to take leave of them: for their
45 joy waded in tears. There was casting up of eyes,
holding up of hands, with countenance of such
distraction that they were to be known by garment,
not by favour. Our king, being ready to leap out of
himself for joy of his found daughter, as if that joy
50 were now become a loss cries 'O, thy mother, thy
mother!'; then asks Bohemia forgiveness; then
embraces his son-in-law; then again worries he his
daughter with clipping her; now he thanks the old
shepherd, which stands by like a weather-bitten
55 conduit of many kings' reigns. I never heard of such
another encounter, which lames report to follow it
and undoes description to do it.

Second Gentleman

What, pray you, became of Antigonus, that carried
hence the child?

Third Gentleman

60 Like an old tale still, which will have matter to
rehearse, though credit be asleep and not an ear
open: he was torn to pieces with a bear. This
avouches the shepherd's son, who has not only his
innocence, which seems much, to justify him, but a
65 handkerchief and rings of his that Paulina knows.

First Gentleman

What became of his bark and his followers?

Third Gentleman

Wracked the same instant of their master's death,
and in the view of the shepherd: so that all the
instruments which aided to expose the child were
70 even then lost when it was found. But O, the noble
combat that 'twixt joy and sorrow was fought in
Paulina! She had one eye declined for the loss of her
husband, another elevated that the oracle was
fulfilled. She lifted the princess from the earth, and
75 so locks her in embracing as if she would pin her to

46 *countenance*: appearance.

48 *favour*: feature.

53 *clipping*: embracing.
54–5 *weather-bitten . . . reigns*: weather-worn
old waterspout which has lasted
throughout the reigns (*and* rains) of
many kings; the image is of a gargoyle
in the form of an old man.

56–7 *lames report . . . to do it*: beats anything
that can follow it and beggars
description to do justice to it.
60–2 *which will . . . open*: which carries on
even when the hearers have exhausted
their capacity for belief and are no
longer listening.
64 *innocence*: simple-mindedness,
guilelessness.

72–3 *one eye . . . another*: To weep with one
eye and laugh with the other was a
proverbial expression (= to experience a
mixture of joy and grief).

77 *losing*: being lost.

81 *angled*: caught.
    the water: i.e. tears.

85 *attentiveness*: listening to this.

88 *Who . . . marble*: the most hard-hearted person.

94 *rare*: talented.

her heart, that she might no more be in danger of losing.

First Gentleman

The dignity of this act was worth the audience of kings and princes, for by such was it acted.

Third Gentleman

80 One of the prettiest touches of all, and that which angled for mine eyes—caught the water though not the fish—was when at the relation of the queen's death, with the manner how she came to't bravely confessed and lamented by the king, how

85 attentiveness wounded his daughter; till, from one sign of dolour to another, she did, with an 'Alas!', I would fain say bleed tears; for I am sure my heart wept blood. Who was most marble there changed colour; some swooned, all sorrowed. If all the world

90 could have seen't, the woe had been universal.

First Gentleman

Are they returned to the court?

Third Gentleman

No: the princess, hearing of her mother's statue, which is in the keeping of Paulina—a piece many years in doing and now newly performed by that rare

95 *Julio Romano*: An Italian artist, famous
    as painter rather than sculptor.

97 *beguile . . . custom*: do Nature out of a
    job.

98 *ape*: imitator, competitor.

100–1 *greediness of affection*: eager desire.

104 *removed*: remote.

105 *piece*: augment, complete.

109 *unthrifty*: careless, wasteful (by losing
    opportunity to improve).

113 *aboard the prince*: i.e. to the prince when
    he was on board ship.

121 *relished*: pleased, done me any good.

125 *gentlemen born*: born already gentlemen
    (because their grandfather has been
    made a gentleman). In Shakespeare's
    day, a person had to be descended from
    three generations of gentry on both
    sides in order to be officially accepted
    as a 'gentleman born'.

128 *clothes*: The saying that 'apparel oft
    proclaims the man' was proverbial.

---

95 Italian master, Julio Romano, who, had he himself
eternity and could put breath into his work, would
beguile Nature of her custom, so perfectly he is her
ape: he so near to Hermione hath done Hermione
that they say one would speak to her and stand in
100 hope of answer. Thither with all greediness of
affection are they gone, and there they intend to sup.

Second Gentleman
I thought she had some great matter there in hand,
for she hath privately, twice or thrice a day, ever
since the death of Hermione, visited that removed
105 house. Shall we thither, and with our company piece
the rejoicing?

First Gentleman
Who would be thence that has the benefit of access?
Every wink of an eye some new grace will be born.
Our absence makes us unthrifty to our knowledge.
110 Let's along.

                      [*Exeunt* Gentlemen

Autolycus
Now, had I not the dash of my former life in me,
would preferment drop on my head. I brought the
old man and his son aboard the prince; told him I
heard them talk of a fardel and I know not what: but
115 he at that time overfond of the shepherd's
daughter—so he then took her to be—who began to
be much sea-sick, and himself little better, extremity
of weather continuing, this mystery remained
undiscovered. But 'tis all one to me; for had I been
120 the finder-out of this secret, it would not have
relished among my other discredits.

Enter Shepherd *and* Clown

Here come those I have done good to against my will,
and already appearing in the blossoms of their fortune.

Shepherd
Come, boy, I am past more children; but thy sons
125 and daughters will be all gentlemen born.

Clown
You are well met, sir. You denied to fight with me
this other day because I was no gentleman born. See
you these clothes? Say you see them not and think

130 *give me the lie*: tell me I'm lying; a
gentleman's honour required him to
fight when accused to his face of lying.

143 *preposterous*: The Clown means
'prosperous'—but his mistaken word i
more apt.

148 *gentle*: generous.

151 *an it like*: if it please.

155 *Not swear . . . gentleman*: Swearing, like
duelling, was held to be a prerogative of
gentlemen.
boors: peasants.
156 *franklins*: yeomen.

130 me still no gentleman born. You were best say these
robes are not gentlemen born. Give me the lie, do,
and try whether I am not now a gentleman born.

Autolycus
I know you are now, sir, a gentleman born.

Clown
Ay, and have been so any time these four hours.

Shepherd
And so have I, boy.

Clown
135 So you have; but I was a gentleman born before my
father: for the king's son took me by the hand, and
called me brother; and then the two kings called my
father brother; and then the prince my brother and
the princess my sister called my father father. And so
140 we wept; and there was the first gentleman-like tears
that ever we shed.

Shepherd
We may live, son, to shed many more.

Clown
Ay, or else 'twere hard luck, being in so preposterous
estate as we are.

Autolycus
145 I humbly beseech you, sir, to pardon me all the faults
I have committed to your worship, and to give me
your good report to the prince my master.

Shepherd
Prithee, son, do: for we must be gentle, now we are
gentlemen.

Clown
150 Thou wilt amend thy life?

Autolycus
Ay, an it like your good worship.

Clown
Give me thy hand. I will swear to the prince thou art
as honest a true fellow as any is in Bohemia.

Shepherd
You may say it, but not swear it.

Clown
155 Not swear it, now I am a gentleman? Let boors and
franklins say it, I'll swear it.

Shepherd
How if it be false, son?

Clown
If it be ne'er so false, a true gentleman may swear it in
the behalf of his friend; and I'll swear to the prince
160 thou art a tall fellow of thy hands, and that thou wilt
not be drunk; but I know thou art no tall fellow of thy
hands, and that thou wilt be drunk. But I'll swear it,
and I would thou wouldst be a tall fellow of thy hands.

Autolycus
I will prove so, sir, to my power.

Clown
165 Ay, by any means prove a tall fellow. If I do not
wonder how thou dar'st venture to be drunk, not
being a tall fellow, trust me not. Hark, the kings and
the princes, our kindred, are going to see the queen's
picture. Come, follow us: we'll be thy good masters.

[Exeunt

160 *tall . . . hands*: valiant fellow in a fight.

163 *I would*: I wish.

164 *to my power*: as well as I can, in my way.
Autolycus has no intention to reform:
he will use his hands as cut-purse and
pick-pocket.

169 *picture*: likeness, effigy.

Act 5   Scene 3

The full company, led by Leontes and
Polixenes, assembles for the unveiling of the
painted statue that Paulina is preparing to
show them. But this is more than an
ordinary statue! With the reunion of
Hermione and Leontes, the play's happy
ending is assured.

1 *grave*: dignified, respected.
4 *home*: in full.
7 *It is . . . grace*: you are more than
   gracious.
9 *with trouble*: by being troublesome to
   you.
12 *singularities*: rare treasures.
18 *Lonely*: isolated.
19 *lively mock'd*: closely imitated.
23 *something near*: fairly close to life.

Scene 3

> *Enter* Leontes, Polixenes, Florizel, Perdita,
> Camillo, Paulina, Lords, *and* Attendants

Leontes
O grave and good Paulina, the great comfort
That I have had of thee!
    Paulina
                What, sovereign sir,
I did not well, I meant well. All my services
You have paid home: but that you have vouchsaf'd,
5 With your crown'd brother and these your contracted
Heirs of your kingdoms, my poor house to visit,
It is a surplus of your grace, which never
My life may last to answer.
    Leontes
                O Paulina,
We honour you with trouble. But we came
10 To see the statue of our queen: your gallery
Have we pass'd through, not without much content
In many singularities; but we saw not
That which my daughter came to look upon,
The statue of her mother.
    Paulina
             As she liv'd peerless,
15 So her dead likeness I do well believe
Excels whatever yet you look'd upon,
Or hand of man hath done; therefore I keep it
Lonely, apart. But here it is: prepare
To see the life as lively mock'd as ever
20 Still sleep mock'd death. Behold, and say 'tis well!

> Paulina *draws a curtain and reveals*
> Hermione, *standing like a statue*

I like your silence: it the more shows off
Your wonder. But yet speak: first you, my liege.
Comes it not something near?
    Leontes
              Her natural posture!
Chide me, dear stone, that I may say indeed
25 Thou art Hermione; or rather, thou art she
In thy not chiding, for she was as tender

As infancy and grace. But yet, Paulina,
Hermione was not so much wrinkled, nothing
So aged as this seems.

Polixenes

                      O, not by much!

Paulina

30 So much the more our carver's excellence,
Which lets go by some sixteen years and makes her
As she liv'd now.

Leontes

               As now she might have done,
So much to my good comfort as it is
Now piercing to my soul. O, thus she stood,
35 Even with such life of majesty—warm life,
As now it coldly stands—when first I woo'd her!
I am asham'd. Does not the stone rebuke me
For being more stone than it? O royal piece!
There's magic in thy majesty, which has
40 My evils conjur'd to remembrance, and
From thy admiring daughter took the spirits,
Standing like stone with thee.

Perdita

                    And give me leave,
And do not say 'tis superstition, that
I kneel and then implore her blessing. Lady,
45 Dear queen, that ended when I but began,
Give me that hand of yours to kiss!

Paulina

                      O, patience!
The statue is but newly fix'd, the colour's
Not dry.

Camillo

My lord, your sorrow was too sore laid on,
50 Which sixteen winters cannot blow away,
So many summers dry. Scarce any joy
Did ever so long live; no sorrow
But kill'd itself much sooner.

Polixenes

                 Dear my brother,
Let him that was the cause of this have power
55 To take off so much grief from you as he
Will piece up in himself.

---

38 *piece*: work of art.

40 *My evils . . . remembrance*: brought to mind my offences.
41 *admiring*: wondering.

47 *The statue . . . fix'd*: the colours of the statue have only just been made fast.

49 *sore*: heavily, thickly; Camillo uses a metaphor from painting, inspired by the preceding lines.

54–6 Polixenes, identifying himself as the root cause of all the trouble, wants to take away some of Leontes' grief by sharing it (compare the proverb, 'a problem shared is a problem halved').
56 *piece up*: parcel, add up.

Paulina

Indeed, my lord,
If I had thought the sight of my poor image
Would thus have wrought you—for the stone is
      mine—
I'd not have show'd it.

Leontes

Do not draw the curtain.

Paulina

60 No longer shall you gaze on't, lest your fancy
May think anon it moves.

Leontes

Let be, let be!
Would I were dead but that methinks already—
What was he that did make it? See, my lord:
Would you not deem it breath'd, and that those veins
65 Did verily bear blood?

Polixenes

Masterly done!
The very life seems warm upon her lip.

Leontes

The fixure of her eye has motion in't
As we are mock'd with art.

Paulina

I'll draw the curtain.
My lord's almost so far transported that
70 He'll think anon it lives.

Leontes

O sweet Paulina,
Make me to think so twenty years together!
No settled senses of the world can match
The pleasure of that madness. Let't alone.

Paulina

I am sorry, sir, I have thus far stirr'd you; but
75 I could afflict you farther.

Leontes

Do, Paulina:
For this affliction has a taste as sweet
As any cordial comfort. Still methinks
There is an air comes from her. What fine chisel
Could ever yet cut breath? Let no man mock me,
80 For I will kiss her.

58   *wrought*: affected, moved.

62   *Would I . . . already*: may I die if I'm not
thinking already that [the statue has
moved].

67   'Just the way her eye has been set
makes it move.' 'Fixure', a technical
term in painting, is also an early form
of 'fixture'—thereby allowing Leontes'
paradox.
68   *As*: in such a way.

72   *settled*: normal.

77   *cordial*: heartwarming.

Paulina

　　　　　　　　　　　　Good my lord, forbear.
The ruddiness upon her lip is wet:
You'll mar it if you kiss it; stain your own
With oily painting. Shall I draw the curtain?

Leontes

No, not these twenty years.

Perdita

　　　　　　　　　　　　　　So long could I
85 Stand by, a looker-on.

Paulina

　　　　　　　　　　　　　Either forbear,
Quit presently the chapel, or resolve you
For more amazement. If you can behold it,
I'll make the statue move indeed, descend
And take you by the hand: but then you'll think—
90 Which I protest against—I am assisted
By wicked powers.

Leontes

　　　　　　　　　　　What you can make her do
I am content to look on; what to speak
I am content to hear; for 'tis as easy
To make her speak as move.

Paulina

　　　　　　　　　　　　　It is requir'd
95 You do awake your faith. Then all stand still;
Or those that think it is unlawful business
I am about, let them depart.

Leontes

　　　　　　　　　　　　　Proceed.
No foot shall stir.

Paulina

　　　　　　　　Music, awake her, strike!

Music

'Tis time: descend; be stone no more; approach;
100 Strike all that look upon with marvel. Come,
I'll fill your grave up. Stir; nay, come away.
Bequeath to death your numbness, for from him
Dear life redeems you. You perceive she stirs.

Hermione *descends*

83 *painting*: paint.

85 *forbear*: withdraw.
86 *presently*: immediately.
87 *can*: i.e. if you think you can.

104 *Start not*: don't be afraid, startled.

Start not: her actions shall be holy as
105 You hear my spell is lawful. [*To* Leontes] Do not
         shun her
Until you see her die again, for then

107 *double*: for a second time.

You kill her double. Nay, present your hand.
When she was young you woo'd her: now, in age,
Is she become the suitor?

Leontes
                              O, she's warm!
110 If this be magic, let it be an art
Lawful as eating.

Polixenes
                              She embraces him.

Camillo
She hangs about his neck.

113 *If she . . . life*: if she's really alive.

If she pertain to life, let her speak too.

Polixenes
Ay, and make it manifest where she has liv'd,
115 Or how stol'n from the dead.

Paulina
                              That she is living,

116 *hooted*: scoffed.

Were it but told you, should be hooted at
Like an old tale: but it appears she lives,
Though yet she speak not. Mark a little while.
[*To* Perdita] Please you to interpose, fair madam;
         kneel,
120 And pray your mother's blessing. Turn, good lady:
Our Perdita is found.

Hermione
                              You gods, look down,
And from your sacred vials pour your graces
Upon my daughter's head! Tell me, mine own,
Where hast thou been preserv'd? Where liv'd? How
         found
125 Thy father's court? For thou shalt hear that I,

126 *Knowing by Paulina*: having learned from Paulina. In fact Hermione herself heard the message from the oracle (3, 2, 137).

Knowing by Paulina that the oracle
Gave hope thou wast in being, have preserv'd
Myself to see the issue.

Paulina
                              There's time enough for that,

129 *upon this push*: at this particular moment.
    trouble: interrupt.
130 *like relation*: the same kind of story.

Lest they desire upon this push to trouble
130 Your joys with like relation. Go together,
You precious winners all; your exultation

132 *Partake to*: share with, make known to.
turtle: turtle dove; a symbol of marital
constancy—see *4, 4, 154 note*.

135 *lost*: lost to life, i.e. dead.

142 *For*: as for.

144 *whose . . . honesty*: Leontes refers to
Camillo.
145 *richly noted*: very well known.
justified: vouched for.
146 *from*: go from.

149 *This'*: this is.

151 *troth-plight*: betrothed; compare *4, 4,
414 note*.

155 *dissever'd*: split up.

Partake to everyone. I, an old turtle,
Will wing me to some wither'd bough, and there
My mate, that's never to be found again,
135 Lament till I am lost.
       Leontes
                O peace, Paulina!
Thou shouldst a husband take by my consent,
As I by thine a wife. This is a match,
And made between's by vows. Thou hast found
    mine—
But how is to be question'd: for I saw her,
140 As I thought, dead; and have in vain said many
A prayer upon her grave. I'll not seek far—
For him, I partly know his mind—to find thee
An honourable husband. Come, Camillo,
And take her by the hand; whose worth and honesty
145 Is richly noted, and here justified
By us, a pair of kings. Let's from this place.
[*To* Hermione] What! Look upon my brother. Both
    your pardons
That e'er I put between your holy looks
My ill suspicion. This' your son-in-law,
150 And son unto the king, whom heavens directing,
Is troth-plight to your daughter. Good Paulina,
Lead us from hence, where we may leisurely
Each one demand and answer to his part
Perform'd in this wide gap of time since first
155 We were dissever'd. Hastily lead away.
                             [*Exeunt*

The Raw Material

Pandosto, or, The Triumph of Time, a prose romance by Robert Greene (first published 1588) supplied Shakespeare with the double plot of *The Winter's Tale*, and gave suggestions for some of the characters. The plots are alike in outline and direction, but Shakespeare made some interesting alterations to Greene's fiction. A comparison of the play with its source can only evoke wonder and admiration for Shakespeare's craftsmanship, but the romance is too long and leisurely to be printed here in its entirety. A summarized comparison is offered now, followed by short passages intended as 'tasters'; interested readers should consult the complete texts which are readily available (see 'Further Reading', p. 148).

Shakespeare switches the locations of the two actions: Greene's Bohemia is Shakespeare's Sicilia, and vice versa. In Greene's narrative Pandosto's jealousy is slower in its development, though no less violent in outcome, than that of Shakespeare's Leontes. Both kings become suspicious of their wives (Bellaria and Hermione) and their boyhood friends (Egistus and Polixenes), accusing them of adultery and conspiracy to murder. Both reject the child born to the imprisoned wife, casting it to the mercy of wind and sea: in *Pandosto* the baby is unaccompanied and drifts aimlessly, but Shakespeare allows Perdita the guardianship of Antigonus and the guidance of his dream-vision. Pandosto succeeds in convincing the whole court of his suspicions; and it is Bellaria who appeals for the judgement of the oracle to prove her innocence. Leontes is alone in his delusions, himself invoking the oracle in the hope of persuading the courtiers of Hermione's guilt.

When the oracle's verdict is delivered to Pandosto, the king is immediately contrite and begs forgiveness: Leontes, on the other hand, blasphemes the god by refusing the judgement. In both stories the oracle's prophecy is followed by news that the king's son is dead, and on hearing this the two queens fall to the ground—but only Bellaria dies indeed.

The interest now turns to the abandoned infant who, having been shipwrecked on a desert shore (Sicilia in Greene's story, Bohemia in Shakespeare's play), is rescued by an old shepherd. She grows up to be a remarkably beautiful and accomplished young woman, and is loved by the king's son, who disguises himself in peasant's clothing to visit her cottage.

Once again, the story outlines are alike—but the details are very different. Greene's shepherd has a wife, and they adopt the child from largely mercenary motives. The wife of Shakespeare's Shepherd does not appear in the play, but the Shepherd and his son, the Clown, are humane men and it seems that they foster the child out of kindness.

In both plays the prince and the shepherdess are very conscious of rank and class. In *Pandosto* Dorastus despises himself for loving a country wench, though Fawnia looks forward to becoming his queen; but in *The Winter's Tale* Perdita chides her lover for deigning to love one of her social level, and warns him that there may be danger in such condescension.

When their betrothed love is threatened, both pairs of lovers—with the aid of resourceful servants—make their escape and, followed by the adoptive fathers of the two 'shepherdesses' and the fathers of the two princes, arrive, respectively, in Bohemia and Sicilia.

In Bohemia Greene's headstrong king seems to have been unaffected by the loss of his wife and children. Encountering the runaway lovers, he casts lustful eyes on Fawnia and commits Dorastus to prison. When the prince's father identifies and pleads for his son, Pandosto, who has hitherto been unreconciled to Egistus, exchanges passion for hatred and threatens Fawnia with torture and death. She is saved only when the old shepherd, himself having been condemned to death, reveals the truth about his finding of her—whereupon the shepherd is knighted and, amidst general rejoicing, the lovers are married. But Pandosto's guilt has been reawakened and, giving an unusual twist to a romance story, he kills himself.

In Sicilia, however, Leontes is a changed man and, when the confusions of mistaken identity are happily resolved, his long penance is richly rewarded through the device of the 'statue', which Shakespeare introduces to enable the completeness of the reconciliation.

Act 1, Scene 2

The queen entertains the royal visitor

'Bellaria . . . who in her time was the flower of courtesy, willing to show how unfeignedly she loved her husband by his friend's entertainment, used him likewise so familiarly that her countenance betrayed how her mind was affected towards him, oftentimes coming herself into his bedchamber to see that nothing should be amiss to mislike him. This honest familiarity increased daily more [until] there grew such a secret uniting of their affections, that the one could not well be without the company of the other: in so much, that when Pandosto was busied with such urgent affairs that he could not be present with his friend Egistus, Bellaria would walk with him to the garden, where they two in private and pleasant devices would pass away the time to both their contents . . .'

Act 2, Scene 2

The king rejects his daughter

'Bellaria was brought to bed of a fair and beautiful daughter, which no sooner Pandosto heard, but he determined that both Bellaria and the young infant should be burnt with fire. His nobles hearing of the king's cruel sentence sought by persuasions to divert him from his bloody determination, . . . [and] at last, seeing his noblemen were importunate upon him, he was content to spare the child's life, and yet to put it to a worser death. For he found out this device, that seeing, as he thought, it came by fortune, so he would commit it to the charge of fortune and, therefore, he caused a little cock-boat to be provided, wherein he meant to put the babe . . .'

Act 3, Scene 2

The queen defends herself

'Bellaria . . . feeling in herself a clear conscience to withstand her false accusers, seeing that no less than death could pacify her husband's wrath, waxed bold and desired that she might have law and justice, for mercy she neither craved nor hoped [for] . . . But Pandosto, whose rage and jealousy was such as no reason nor equity could appease, told her that, for her accusers, they were of such credit as their words were sufficient witness, and that the sudden and secret flight of Egistus and Franion confirmed that which they had confessed; and as for her, it was her part to deny such a monstrous crime, and to be impudent in forswearing the fact, since she had passed all shame in committing the fault but her stale countenance should stand for no coin, for as the bastard which she bare was served, so she should with some cruel death be requitted. Bellaria, no whit dismayed with this rough reply, told her husband Pandosto that he spake upon choler and not conscience, for her virtuous life had been ever such as no spot of suspicion could ever stain. And if she had borne a friendly countenance to Egistus, it was in respect he was his friend and not for any lusting affection; therefore, if she were condemned without further proof it was rigour and not law.'

Act 4, Scene 2

The prince loves the shepherdess

'Dorastus . . . could not by any means forget the sweet favour of Fawnia, . . . [but] he began with divers considerations to suppress his frantic affection, calling to mind that Fawnia was a shepherd, one not worthy to be looked at of a prince, much less to be loved by such a potentate; thinking what a discredit it were to himself, and what a grief it would be to his father, blaming fortune and accusing his own folly that should be so fond as but once to cast a glance at such a country slut . . .'

'. . . he presently made himself a shepherd's coat, that he might go unknown and with the less suspicion to prattle with Fawnia, and conveyed it secretly to a thick grove hard joining to the palace . . . But, as he went by the way, seeing himself clad in such unseemly rags, he began to smile at his own folly and reprove his fondness in these terms. . . . And yet, Dorastus, shame not at thy shepherd's weed. The heavenly gods have sometime earthly thoughts. Neptune became a ram, Jupiter a bull, Apollo a shepherd: they gods, and yet in love; and thou a man appointed to love . . .'

The shepherdess speaks to the prince

'Ah, Dorastus, I shame to express that thou forcest me with thy sugared speech to confess: my base birth causeth the one, and thy high dignities the other. Beggars' thoughts ought not to reach so far as kings, and yet my desires reach as high as princes. . . .'

What the Critics have said

Samuel Johnson

'. . . It was, I suppose, only to spare his own labour that the poet put this whole scene into narrative, for though part of the transaction was already known to the audience, and therefore could not properly be shewn again, yet the two kings might have met upon the stage, and after examination of the old shepherd, the young Lady might have been recognised in sight of the spectators.'

A note on Act 5, Scene 3, from *The Plays of William Shakespeare* (1765)

William Hazlitt

'*The Winter's Tale* is one of the best-acting of our author's plays. We remember seeing it with great pleasure many years ago . . . Mrs Siddons played Hermione, and in the last scene acted the painted statue to the life—with true monumental dignity and noble passion; Mr Kemble, in Leontes, worked himself up into a very fine classical phrensy; and Bannister, as Autolycus, roared as loud for pity as a sturdy beggar could do who felt none of the pain he counterfeited, and was sound of wind and limb. We shall never see these parts so acted again; or if we did, it would be in vain. Actors grow old, or no longer surprise us by their novelty. But true poetry, like nature, is always young; and we still read the courtship of Florizel and Perdita, as we welcome the return of spring, with the same feelings as ever.'

Characters of Shakespeare's Plays (1817)

S.T. Coleridge

'The idea of this delightful drama is a genuine jealousy of disposition, and it should be immediately followed by the perusal of *Othello*, which is the direct contrast of it in every particular. For jealousy is a vice of the mind, a culpable tendency of the temper, having certain well known and well defined effects and concomitants, all of which are visible in Leontes, and, I boldly say, not one of which marks its presence in *Othello*;—such as, first, an excitability by the most inadequate causes, and an eagerness to snatch at proofs; secondly, a grossness of conception, and a disposition to degrade the object of the passion by sensual fancies and images; thirdly, a sense of shame of his own feelings exhibited in a solitary moodiness of humour, and yet from the violence of the passion forced to utter itself, and therefore catching occasions to ease the mind by ambiguities, equivoques, by talking to those who cannot, and who are known not to be able to, understand what is said to them,—in short, by soliloquy in the form of dialogue, and hence a confused, broken, and fragmentary manner; fourthly, a dread of vulgar ridicule, as distinct from a high sense of honour, or a mistaken sense of duty; and lastly, and immediately consequent on this, a spirit of selfish vindictiveness.'

From the notes of a lecture (1818)

Anna Jameson

'The character of Hermione exhibits what is never found in the other sex, but rarely in our own,—yet sometimes,—dignity without pride, love without passion, and tenderness without weakness. To conceive a character, in which there enters so much of the negative, required perhaps no rare and astonishing effort of genius . . . but to delineate such a character in a poetical form, to develop it through the medium of action and dialogue, without the aid of description; to preserve its tranquil, mild and serious beauty, its unimpassioned dignity, and at the same time keep the strongest hold upon our sympathy and our imagination; and out of this exterior calm, produce the most profound pathos, the most vivid impression of life and internal power:—it is this, which renders the character of Hermione one of Shakespeare's masterpieces.'

Shakespeare's Heroines (1833)

Hartley Coleridge

'Except for Autolycus, none of the characters shows anything of Shakespeare's philosophic depth. . . . Hermione is frank and noble, rising in dignity as she falls in fortune . . . in sunshine a butterfly, in misery a martyr. Paulina is an honest scold. Perdita a pretty piece of poetry. Polixenes is not very amiable, nor, in truth, much of anything. The length of time he remains witness to his son's courtship, before he discovers himself, is a sacrifice to effect. Camillo is an old rogue whom I can hardly forgive for his double treachery. The shepherd and his son are well enough in their way; but Mopsa and Dorcas might be countrified enough with better tongues in their heads. Of the rest nothing need be said.'

Essays and Marginalia (1851)

Sir Arthur Quiller-Couch

'This brings us to the greatest fault of all; to the recognition scene; or rather to the scamping of it. To be sure, if we choose to tread foot with Gervinus and agree that "the poet has *wisely* placed this event behind the scenes, otherwise the play would have been too full of powerful scenes"; if, having been promised a mighty thrill, in the great master's fashion, we really prefer two or three innominate gentlemen entering and saying, "Have you heard?" "You don't tell me!" "No?" "Then you have lost a sight"—I say, if we really prefer this sort of thing, which Gervinus calls "in itself a rare masterpiece of prose description", then Heaven must be our aid. But if, using our own judgement, we read the play and put ourselves in the place of its first audience, I ask, Are we not baulked? In proportion as we have paid tribute to the art of the story by letting our interest be intrigued, our emotion excited, are we not cheated when Shakespeare lets us down with this reported tale? I would point out that it nowise resembles the Messengers' tales in Greek tragedy. These related bloody deeds, things not to be displayed on the stage.'

Shakespeare's Workmanship (1915)

Harold C. Goddard

'The defeat of death is the main problem of humanity. That defeat may be affected either by the direct imitation of divinity by man (the way of religion) or by the indirect imitation of it through the creation of divine works (the way of art), though practically it must be a combination of the two, for it is only the religion that speaks artistically that is articulate and only the art that is pervaded by a religious spirit that is redeeming. As Perdita impersonated the goddess Flora, so Hermione imitates an artistic incarnation of herself as a work of sculpture. Sixteen years in which to rehearse the effect of adversity on love have made her a living proof of her daughter's words in her own moment of adversity:

> I think affliction may subdue the cheek
> But not take in the mind.'

The Meaning of Shakespeare (1951)

Hermione Speaks

Helen Faucit, Lady Martin: An Actress Describes her Part

Act 5, Scene 3

'I never approached this scene without much inward trepidation. You may imagine how difficult it must be to stand in one position, with a full light thrown upon you, without moving an eyelid for so long a time. I never thought to have the time measured, but I should say it must be more than ten minutes,—it seemed like ten times ten. . . .

Paulina had, it seemed to me, besought Hermione to play the part of her own statue, in order that she might hear herself apostrophised, and be a silent witness of the remorse and unabated love of Leontes before her existence became known to him, and so be moved to that forgiveness which, without such proof, she might possibly be slow to yield. She is so moved; but for the sake of the loving friend, to whom she has owed so much, she must restrain herself, and carry through her appointed task. But, even although I had fully thought out all this, it was impossible for me ever to hear unmoved what passes in this wonderful scene. My first Leontes was Mr Macready, and, as the scene was played by him, the difficulty of wearing an air of statuesque calm became almost insuperable. As I think over the scene now, his appearance, his action, the tones of his voice, the emotions of the time, come back. There was a dead awe-struck silence when the curtains were gradually drawn aside by Paulina. She has to encourage Leontes to speak. . . .

Never can I forget the manner in which Mr Macready here cried out, "Do not draw the curtain" and, afterwards, "Let be, let be!" in tones irritable, commanding, and impossible to resist. "Would I were dead," he continues, "but that, methinks, already—" Has he seen something that makes him think the statue lives? Mr Macready indicated this, and hurriedly went on "What was he", etc. His eyes have been so riveted upon the figure, that he sees what the others have not seen, that there is something about it beyond the reach of art. . . .

You may conceive the relief I felt when the first strain of solemn music set me free to breathe! There was a pedestal by my side on which I leant. It was a slight help during the long strain upon the nerves and muscles, besides allowing me to stand in that "natural posture" which first strikes Leontes, and which therefore could not have been rigidly statuesque. By imperceptibly altering the poise of the body, the weight of it being on the forward foot, I could drop into the easiest position from which to move. The hand and arm still resting quietly on the pedestal materially helped me. Towards the close of the strain the head slowly turned, the "full eyes" moved, and at the last note rested on Leontes. This movement, together with the expression of the face, transfigured as we may have imagined it to have been, by years of sorrow and devout meditation,—speechless, yet saying things unutterable,— always produced a startling, magnetic effect upon all,—the audience upon the stage as well as in front of it.

After the burst of amazement had hushed down, at a sign from Paulina the solemn sweet strain recommenced. The arm and hand were gently lifted from the pedestal; then, rhythmically following the music, the figure descended the steps that led up to the dais, and advancing slowly, paused at a short distance from Leontes. Oh, can I ever forget Mr Macready at this point! At first he stood speechless, as if turned to stone; his face with an awe-struck look upon it. Could this, the very counterpart of his queen, be a wondrous piece of mechanism? Could art so mock the life? He had seen her laid out as dead, the funeral obsequies performed over her, with her dear son beside her. Thus absorbed in wonder, he remained until Paulina said, "Nay, present your hand." Tremblingly he advanced, and touched gently the hand held out to him. Then what a cry came with, "O, she's warm!"

It is impossible to describe Mr Macready here. He was Leontes' very self. His passionate joy at finding Hermione really alive seemed beyond control. Now he was prostrate at her feet, then enfolding her in his arms. I had a slight veil or covering over my head and neck, supposed to make the statue look older. This fell off in an instant. The hair, which came unbound, and fell on my shoulders, was reverently kissed and caressed. The whole change was so sudden, so overwhelming, that I suppose I cried out hysterically, for he whispered to me, "Don't be frightened, my child! don't be frightened! Control yourself!"

All this went on during a tumult of applause that sounded like a storm of hail. Oh, how glad I was to be released, when, as soon as a lull came, Paulina, advancing with Perdita, said, "Turn, good lady, our Perdita is found." A broken, trembling voice, I am sure, was mine, as I said, "You gods, look down," etc. It was such a comfort to me as well as true to natural feeling, that Shakespeare gives no word to Hermione to say to Leontes, but leaves her to assure him of her joy and forgiveness by look and manner only, as in his arms she feels the old life, so long suspended, come back to her again. . . .'

On Some of Shakespeare's Female Characters (1891)

Songs in *The Winter's Tale*

Jog on, jog on the footpath way

Act 4, Scene 3

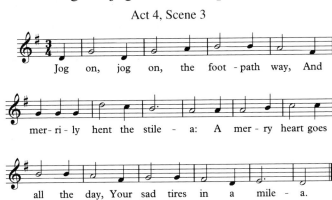

Jog on, jog on, the foot - path way, And

mer - ri - ly hent the stile - a: A mer - ry heart goes

all the day, Your sad tires in a mile - a.

Lawn as white as driven snow

Act 4, Scene 4

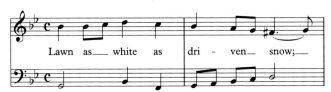

Lawn as— white as dri - ven— snow;—

Cy - press black— as e'er— was— crow;

Gloves as sweet as da - mask— ro - ses;—

Masks for fa - ces,— and— for no - ses;

Bu - gle - brace - let, neck - lace -

Get you hence, for I must go

Act 4, Scene 4

Classwork and Examinations

The plays of Shakespeare are studied all over the world, and this classroom edition is being used in many different countries—and often in countries where English is not the students' first language. Teaching methods vary from school to school, and there are many different ways of examining a student's work. Some teachers and examiners expect detailed knowledge of Shakespeare's text, others ask for imaginative involvement with his characters and their situations; and there are some teachers who want their students to share in the theatrical experience of directing and performing a play. Most people use a variety of methods. This section of the book offers a few suggestions for approaches to *The Winter's Tale* which could be used in schools and colleges to help with students' understanding and *enjoyment* of the play.

    A Discussion
    B Character Study
    C Activities
    D Context Questions
    E Comprehension Questions
    F Essays
    G Projects

A   Discussion

Talking about the play—about the issues it raises and the characters who are involved—is one of the most rewarding and pleasurable ways of studying Shakespeare. It makes sense to discuss each scene as it is read, sharing impressions—and perhaps correcting misapprehensions. It can be useful to compare aspects of this play with other fictions—plays, novels, films—or with modern life. A large class can divide into small groups, each with a leader, who can discuss different aspects of a single topic and then report back to the main assembly.

Suggestions

A1   Fantasy fiction—is it just a waste of time? Consider the stories you know, the films you have seen, and the books you have read recently as well as the fairy stories you remember from childhood. What use are they? What kind of pleasure do they give?

A2 We were as twinn'd lambs that did frisk i'th'sun
And bleat the one at th'other. What we chang'd
Was innocence for innocence: we knew not
The doctrine of ill-doing, nor dreamed
That any did.

(1, 2, 67–71)

Discuss this view of childhood. Can you think of your own early years (when you were, say, 6 or 7) in these terms? Would it be wise for today's children to be so trusting? Talk to the adults close to you at home, and bring their ideas to share with the class.

A3 How would you stage the episode in *Act 1*, Scene 2 where Leontes' suspicions are aroused when Hermione speaks with Polixenes?

A4 Have you ever been jealous? Can you share your experience with others, and describe the effects of the emotion? Did you overcome your feelings—how?

A5 Perdita is essentially an aristocrat, and being brought up in a humble cottage has not altered her nature:

nothing she does or seems
But smacks of something greater than herself,
Too noble for this place.

(4, 4, 157–9)

What are your views on nature *v.* nurture, birth *v.* breeding (= upbringing), home *v.* school?

A6 Polixenes is in favour of 'artistic' gardening, telling Perdita that

we marry
A gentler scion to the wildest stock,
And make conceive a bark of baser kind
By bud of nobler race.

(4, 4, 92–5)

How far do you go along with the ideas of 'genetic engineering' in plants—and animals?

A7   This is an art
         Which does mend Nature—change it, rather—but
         The art itself is Nature

                                                              (4, 4, 95–7)

Extend Polixenes' argument to human beings and their use of cosmetics, 'cosmetic surgery', and even more radical attempts to 'mend Nature'.

A8   Referring to Autolycus, the Clown and his father observe, 'We are blest in this man', and, 'He was provided to do us good' *(4, 4, 821,824)*. Do *you* believe in Providence?

A9   Do as the heavens have done, forget your evil;
         With them, forgive yourself.

                                                              (5, 1, 5–6)

What are your thoughts about forgiveness? Does it have to be earned—and if so, how? Is it possible to forgive *without* forgetting? Is it easy to forgive *yourself*?

A10 How would you present this play on stage? What setting can you imagine for Sicilia and Bohemia? How would you dress the characters?

B   Character Study

Shakespeare is famous for his creation of characters who seem like real people. We can judge their actions and we can try to comprehend their thoughts and feelings—just as we criticize and try to understand the people we know. As the play progresses, we learn to like or dislike them—just as though they lived in *our* world.

   Characters can be studied *from the outside*, by observing what they do and listening sensitively to what they say. This is the scholar's method: the scholar—or any reader—has access to the entire play, and can see the function of every character within the whole scheme of that play.

   Another approach works *from the inside*, taking a single character and looking at the action and the other characters from his/her point of view. This is the way an actor prepares for performance, creating a personality who can have only a partial notion of what is going on, and it asks for a student's inventive imagination and creative writing. The two methods—both useful in different ways—are really complementary to each other, and for both of them it can be very helpful to re-frame the character's speeches *in your own words*, using the vocabulary and idiom of everyday parlance.

Suggestions

a) from 'outside' the character

B1 Chart the progress of Leontes' jealousy from its first beginnings in *Act 1*, Scene 1.

B2 Trace the development in Hermione's character from her first appearance as a happy wife until she defends herself against her husband's accusations of adultery and conspiracy.

B3 'Leontes is no more than a case-study in obsessive mania; the only credible characters in *The Winter's Tale* are the female ones.'

Either (a) give a considered, critical judgement on this opinion of Leontes;
Or (b) write a detailed character-study of any one of these women:

i) Hermione
ii) Paulina
iii) Perdita

B4 Compare the relationship of Leontes and Hermione with that between Paulina and Antigonus.

B5 'Autolycus was no mere accident: his presence is essential for the operation of the play's mechanism.' Piece together the different aspects of the life of Autolycus, and comment on his function in the play.

b) from 'inside' the character

B6 Archidamus is most appreciative of the reception and entertainment offered to Polixenes in Sicilia, and he reports the details back to Bohemia. Write his report, *either* in a letter to his family and friends; *or* in an article for the national newspaper.

B7 Leontes keeps a diary, recording all that he sees—or *thinks* he sees—that makes him suspicious of his wife and Polixenes.

B8 Whilst his servants are packing for the flight from Sicilia, Polixenes (fearing for his own safety) writes a note to Hermione and a letter to his own son in Bohemia.

B9 In the 'flatness of [her] misery', Hermione tries to express herself in poetry. Attempt one of the following:

    i) Prayer for my Daughter
    ii) On the Death of her First Son
    iii) De Profundis—a lament from the depths of despair
    iv) 'Be still, my soul': a prayer for patience
    v) 'We'll meet again': a song of hope.

B10 The spiritual journal (in verse or prose) of Leontes during his sixteen years of striving to come to terms with his situation.

B11 On days when they can't meet, Florizel writes poetry. Remembering his fondness for classical allusion, compose one (or more) of his poems.

B12 Perdita worries about the difference in social status between herself and Florizel. Write her letters to various newspaper 'agony aunts'—and the replies she might receive (e.g. from 'Aunt Paulina' of the *Mediterranean News*).

B13 Gloves as sweet as damask roses,
    Masks for faces and for noses . . .

Improvise a 'spiel' for a twentieth-century salesman.

B14 ''Tis time!' Paulina's call brings Hermione back into the action—but what thoughts are passing through Hermione's mind whilst she waits for her cue? As Hermione, *or* as the actress playing the part of Hermione, give expression to your thoughts and feelings in a 'stream-of-consciousness' narrative.

B15 Perdita speaks no words to her new-found father but pours out her heart in her diary. Write this confidential journal.

C   Activities

These can involve two or more students, preferably working *away from* the desk or study-table. They can help students to develop a sense of drama and the dramatic aspects of Shakespeare's play— which was written to be *performed*, not read!

C1   Act the play—or at least part of it!

C2 A twentieth-century Hermione questions her husband's friend about the time 'when you were two little boys'.

C3   The scandal!

> They're here with me already: whispering, rounding
> 'Sicilia is a so-forth' . . .

(1, 2, 217–8)

Improvise scenes for the Gentlemen at Leontes' court, and for the Ladies ('Yond crickets', 2, 1, 31), to gossip/argue/speculate about what they have seen and heard.

C4   Nowadays the public trial of a member of the royal family would attract much media attention. Provide such cover—newspaper, radio, and television. Get any interviews you can with persons immediately concerned (? a statement from the palace)—and if you (the journalist) draw a blank here, try absolutely anybody else! Publish letters from readers/viewers arguing both for and against such exposure of the private lives of public figures.

C5   This is the prettiest low-born lass that ever
> Ran on the greensward: nothing she does or seems
> But smacks of something greater than herself,
> Too noble for this place.

(4, 4, 156–9)

Perdita's manners are approved by Polixenes and Camillo—but what do the country folk think of this girl? Devise these episodes:

  i) The Shepherd and the Clown (and perhaps the Shepherd's late wife) speculate about the 'changeling' (3, 3, 115).
  ii) Mopsa and Dorcas tittle-tattle in the kiln-hole, or at bedtime (4, 4, 245), about their own boyfriends and about the strange boy that Perdita has brought home.
  iii) Mopsa and Dorcas (and any other friends) can't stop talking about the excitement of the sheep-shearing feast.

C6   'Such a deal of wonder is broken out within this hour that ballad-makers cannot be able to express it.' (5, 2, 24–5).

Produce a collection of ballads on different aspects of the 'wonder', written by different authors, to be sung and sold to the people of Bohemia. Use as many different idioms as possible (not forgetting rap).

C7   Shakespeare disappointed some of his critics (see p. 122) by 'reporting' two episodes. Supply these:

    i) 'the opening of the fardel'
    ii) 'the meeting of the two kings'.

C8 After all these amazing revelations, Perdita will need to sort out her emotions by talking to a sympathetic listener—Paulina, perhaps. Create this scene.

D   Context Questions

In written examinations, these questions present you with short passages from the play, and ask you to explain them. They are intended to test your knowledge of the play and your understanding of its words. Usually you have to make a choice of passages: there may be five on the paper, and you are asked to choose three. Be very sure that you know exactly how many passages you must choose. Study the ones offered to you, and select those you feel most certain of. Make your answers accurate and concise—don't waste time writing more than the examiner is asking for.

D1   Shall I live on to see this bastard kneel
    And call me father? Better burn it now
    Than curse it then. But be it: let it live.
    It shall not neither. You, sir, come you hither.

    (i) Who is the speaker, and where does he live?
    (ii) Where is 'this bastard' brought up, and under what name?
  (iii) Who is addressed as 'You, sir'?
  (iv) What is he commanded to do?

D2   Thou shalt accompany us to the place, where we will, not appearing what we are, have some question with the shepherd; from whose simplicity I think it not uneasy to get the cause of my son's resort thither.

    (i) Who is spoken to here, and by whom?
    (ii) Where are they going?
  (iii) What is the name of the son who is referred to?
  (iv) What is the reason for his 'resort thither'?

D3   But that your youth
    And the true blood which peeps fairly through't
    Do plainly give you out an unstain'd shepherd,
    With wisdom I might fear, my ——,
    You wooed me the false way.

    (i) Who is the speaker, and where was the speaker born?

(ii) On what occasion is she speaking, and in what country?
(iii) What is the name taken by the 'unstain'd shepherd'
('——'), and what is his real name?

D4 Your changed complexions are to me a mirror
Which shows me mine changed too: for I must be
A party to this alteration, finding
Myself thus altered with't.

(i) Who is speaking, and whose face is 'changed'?
(ii) Of what is the speaker suspected? Who else is accused?
(iii) Where will the speaker go next?

E   Comprehension Questions

These also present passages from the play and ask questions about
them; again you often have a choice of passages. But the extracts
are much longer than those presented as context questions. A
detailed knowledge of the language of the play is required here, and
you must be able to express unusual or archaic phrases in your own
words; you may also be asked to comment critically on the effec-
tiveness of Shakespeare's language.

E1 These dangerous, unsafe lunes i'th'king, beshrew them!
He must be told on't, and he shall. The office
Becomes a woman best. I'll take't upon me.
If I prove honey-mouth'd, let my tongue blister,
And never to my red-look'd anger be   5
The trumpet any more. Pray you, Emilia,
Commend my best obedience to the queen.
If she dares trust me with her little babe,
I'll show't to the king, and undertake to be
Her advocate to th'loud'st. We do not know   10
How he may soften at the sight o'th'child:
The silence often of pure innocence
Persuades when speaking fails.

(i) What is the meaning of 'lunes' (line 1); 'take't upon me'
(line 3); 'honey-mouth'd' (line 4)?
(ii) Express in your own words the sense of lines 4–6, 'let my
tongue . . . any more'; lines 9–10, 'undertake . . . loud'st';
lines 12–13, 'The silence . . . fails'.
(iii) What do these lines reveal of the character of the speaker?
(iv) Comment on the frequency of the elisions (*i'th'*, *on't*,
take't) in this speech.

E2   Too hot, too hot!
　　To mingle friendship far is mingling bloods.
　　I have *tremor cordis* on me: my heart dances,
　　But not for joy, not joy. This entertainment
　　May a free face put on, derive a liberty   5
　　From heartiness, from bounty, fertile bosom,
　　And well become the agent—'t may, I grant.
　　But to be paddling palms and pinching fingers,
　　As now they are, and making practis'd smiles
　　As in a looking glass; and then to sigh, as 'twere   10
　　The mort o'th'deer—O, that is entertainment
　　My bosom likes not, nor my brows!

(i) What is '*tremor cordis*'?
(ii) Explain the meaning of line 2, 'To mingle . . . bloods'; line 11, 'mort o'th'deer'; line 12, 'brows'.
(iii) Express in your own words the sense of lines 4–6, 'This entertainment . . . heartiness'; and line 8, 'paddling . . . fingers'.
(iv) Attempt to explain the state of the speaker's mind as it is expressed in the verse.

F   Essays

These will usually give you a specific topic to discuss, or perhaps a question that must be answered, in writing, *with a reasoned argument*. They *never* want you to tell the story of the play—so don't! Your examiner—or teacher—has read the play, and does not need to be reminded of it. Relevant quotations will always help you to make your points more strongly.

F1   Sicilia and Bohemia seem to be worlds apart: their kings 'Shake hands, as 'twere, over a vast'. How successful is Shakespeare in bringing them together?

F2   There are flaws in every one of the male characters in *The Winter's Tale*: only the women are wholly praiseworthy. Discuss.

F3   Irony and ambiguity in the *The Winter's Tale*.

F4   '*Exit, pursued by a bear*': is this famous stage-direction a sign that Shakespeare is desperate to give his character a way out? Discuss the 'mechanics' of *The Winter's Tale*.

F5   Comment on the use of disguise in *The Winter's Tale*.

F6 Explain what you understand by the observation that 'Perdita's is a destiny to which she must be brought, not travel of her own volition' (Molly Mahood).

F7 Do you agree that 'Too much is left to Chance in *The Winter's Tale*'?

F8 'Shakespeare does not astonish the careful reader: he prepares the way for all the surprises.' How true is this?

G   Projects

In some schools, students are asked to do more 'free-ranging' work, which takes them outside the text—but which should always be relevant to the play. Such Projects may demand skills other than reading and writing: design and artwork, for instance, may be involved. Sometimes a 'portfolio' of work is assembled over a considerable period of time; and this can be offered to the examiner for assessment.

The availability of resources will, obviously, do much to determine the nature of the Projects; but this is something that only the local teachers will understand. However, there is always help to be found in libraries, museums, and art galleries.

Suggested Subjects

G1 Great actors and actresses in *The Winter's Tale*.
G2 Childhood in the early seventeenth century.
G3 Shakespeare's flowers and their symbolism.
G4 Shakespeare's classical mythology.
G5 English country festivals.

Background

England c. 1611

When Shakespeare was writing *The Winter's Tale*, many people still believed that the sun went round the earth. They were taught that this was a divinely ordered scheme of things, and that—in England—God had instituted a Church and ordained a Monarchy for the right government of the land and the populace.

'The past is a foreign country; they do things differently there.'

L. P. Hartley

Government

For most of Shakespeare's life, the reigning monarch of England was Queen Elizabeth I: when she died, she was succeeded by King James I. He was also king of Scotland (James VI), and the two kingdoms were united in 1603 by his accession to the English throne. With his counsellors and ministers, James governed the nation (population less than six million) from London, although fewer than half a million people inhabited the capital city. In the rest of the country, law and order were maintained by the land-owners and enforced by their deputies. The average man had no vote, and his wife had no rights at all.

Religion

At this time, England was a Christian country. All children were baptized, soon after they were born, into the Church of England; they were taught the essentials of the Christian faith, and instructed in their duty to God and to humankind. Marriages were performed, and funerals conducted, only by the licensed clergy and in accordance with the Church's rites and ceremonies. Attendance at divine service was compulsory; absences (without good—medical—reason) could be punished by fines. By such means, the authorities were able to keep some check on the populace—recording births, marriages, and deaths; being alert to any religious nonconformity, which could be politically dangerous; and ensuring a minimum of orthodox instruction through the official 'Homilies' which were regularly preached from the pulpits of all parish churches throughout the realm.

Following Henry VIII's break away from the Church of Rome, all people in England were able to hear the church services *in their own language*. The Book of Common Prayer was used in every church, and an English translation of the Bible was read aloud in public. The Christian religion had never been so well taught before!

Education

School education reinforced the Church's teaching. From the age of four, boys might attend the 'petty school' (French '*petite école*') to learn the rudiments of reading and writing along with a few prayers; some schools also included work with numbers. At the age of seven, the boy was ready for the grammar school (if his father was willing and able to pay the fees).

Here, a thorough grounding in Latin grammar was followed by translation work and the study of Roman authors, paying attention as much to style as to matter. The arts of fine writing were thus inculcated from early youth. A very few students proceeded to university; these were either clever scholarship boys, or else the sons of noblemen. Girls stayed at home, and acquired domestic and social skills—cooking, sewing, perhaps even music. The lucky ones might learn to read and write.

Language

At the start of the sixteenth century the English had a very poor opinion of their own language: there was little serious writing in English, and hardly any literature. Latin was the language of international scholarship, and Englishmen admired the eloquence of the Romans. They made many translations, and in this way they extended the resources of their own language, increasing its vocabulary and stretching its grammatical structures. French, Italian, and Spanish works were also translated and, for the first time, there were English versions of the Bible. By the end of the century, English was a language to be proud of: it was rich in synonyms, capable of infinite variety and subtlety, and ready for all kinds of word-play—especially the *puns*, for which Elizabethan English is renowned.

Drama

The great art-form of the Elizabethan and Jacobean age was its drama. The Elizabethans inherited a tradition of play-acting from the Middle Ages, and they reinforced this by reading and translating the Roman playwrights. At the beginning of the sixteenth century plays were performed by groups of actors, all-male companies (boys acted the female roles) who travelled from town to town, setting up their stages in open places (such as inn-yards) or, with the permission of the owner, in the hall of some noble house. The touring companies continued in the provinces into the seventeenth century; but in London, in 1576, a new building was erected for the performance of plays. This was the Theatre, the first purpose-built playhouse in England. Other playhouses followed, (including the Globe, where most of Shakespeare's plays were performed), and the English drama reached new heights of eloquence.

There were those who disapproved, of course. The theatres, which brought large crowds together, could encourage the spread of disease—and dangerous ideas. During the summer, when the plague was at its worst, the playhouses were closed. A constant censorship was imposed, more or less severe at different times. The Puritan faction tried to close down the theatres, but—partly because there was royal favour for the drama, and partly because the buildings were outside the city limits—they did not succeed until 1642.

Theatre

From contemporary comments and sketches—most particularly a drawing by a Dutch visitor, Johannes de Witt—it is possible to form some idea of the typical Elizabethan playhouse for which most of Shakespeare's plays were written. Hexagonal in shape, it had three roofed galleries encircling an open courtyard. The plain, high stage projected into the yard, where it was surrounded by the audience of standing 'groundlings'. At the back were two doors for the actors' entrances and exits; and above these doors was a balcony—useful for a musicians' gallery or for the acting of scenes 'above'. Over the stage was a thatched roof, supported on two pillars, forming a canopy—which seems to have been painted with the sun, moon, and stars for the 'heavens'.

Underneath was space (concealed by curtaining) which could be used by characters ascending and descending through a trap-door in the stage. Costumes and properties were kept backstage, in the 'tiring house'. The actors dressed lavishly, often wearing the secondhand clothes bestowed by rich patrons. Stage properties were important for defining a location, but the dramatist's own words were needed to explain the time of day, since all performances took place in the early afternoon.

Suggested Further Reading

Barber, C.L., ' "Thou that beget'st him that did thee beget": Transformation in *Pericles* and *The Winter's Tale*', *Shakespeare Survey 22*, (1969), pp. 56–67.

Barton, Anne, 'Leontes and the Spider: Language and Speaker in Shakespeare's Last Plays', *Shakespeare's Styles: Essays in Honour of Kenneth Muir*, ed. Philip Edwards *et al.* (Cambridge, 1980), pp. 131–50.

—— 'Shakespeare and the Limits of Language', *Shakespeare Survey 24* (1971), pp. 19–30.

Bethell, S.L., *The Winter's Tale: A Study*, (London, 1947).

Bullough, Geoffrey, *Narrative and Dramatic Sources of Shakespeare*, vol. 8, (London, 1957–75).

Edwards, Philip, 'Shakespeare's Romances: 1900–1957', *Shakespeare Survey 11*, (1958), 1–18.

Frye, Northrop, *A Natural Perspective: The Development of Shakespearean Comedy and Romance*, (New York, 1955).

Hunter, R.G., *Shakespeare and the Comedy of Forgiveness*, (New York, 1965).

Kermode, Frank, *Shakespeare and the Final Plays*, (Writers and Their Work Series, 155; London, 1963).

Muir, Kenneth, *The Sources of Shakespeare's Plays*, (London, 1977).

Muir, Kenneth (ed.), *Shakespeare: 'The Winter's Tale': a selection of critical essays*, (Casebook Series; London, 1968).

Nuttall, A.D., *William Shakespeare: 'The Winter's Tale'*, (Studies in English Literature, 26; London, 1966).

Pafford, J.H.P. (ed.), *The Winter's Tale*, (Arden Shakespeare, London, 1963).

Pettet, E.C., *Shakespeare and the Romance Tradition*, (London, 1949).

Smith, Jonathan, 'The Language of Leontes', *Shakespeare Quarterly 19* (1968), 317–27.

Tillyard, E.M.W., *Shakespeare's Last Plays*, (London, 1938).

Traversi, Derek A., *Shakespeare: The Last Phase*, (London, 1954).

Wells, Stanley, 'Shakespeare and Romance', in *Later Shakespeare*, ed. John Russell Brown and Bernard Harris (Stratford-upon-Avon Studies, 8; London, 1966), 49–79.

Further Background Reading

Blake, N. F., *Shakespeare's Language: an Introduction*, (London, 1983).

Muir, K., and Schoenbaum, S., *A New Companion to Shakespeare Studies*, (Cambridge, 1971).

Schoenbaum, S., *William Shakespeare: A Documentary Life*, (Oxford, 1975).

Thomson, Peter, *Shakespeare's Theatre*, (London, 1983).

William Shakespeare, 1564–1616

Elizabeth I was Queen of England when Shakespeare was born in 1564. He was the son of a tradesman who made and sold gloves in the small town of Stratford-upon-Avon, and he was educated at the grammar school in that town. Shakespeare did not go to university when he left school, but worked, perhaps, in his father's business. When he was eighteen he married Anne Hathaway, who became the mother of his daughter, Susanna, in 1583, and of twins in 1585.

There is nothing exciting, or even unusual, in this story; and from 1585 until 1592 there are no documents that can tell us anything at all about Shakespeare. But we have learned that in 1592 he was known in London, and that he had become both an actor and a playwright.

We do not know when Shakespeare wrote his first play, and indeed we are not sure of the order in which he wrote his works. If you look on page 152 at the list of his writings and their approximate dates, you will see how he started by writing plays on subjects taken from the history of England. No doubt this was partly because he was always an intensely patriotic man—but he was also a very shrewd business-man. He could see that the theatre audiences enjoyed being shown their own history, and it was certain that he would make a profit from this kind of drama.

The plays in the next group are mainly comedies, with romantic love-stories of young people who fall in love with one another, and at the end of the play marry and live happily ever after.

At the end of the sixteenth century the happiness disappears, and Shakespeare's plays become melancholy, bitter, and tragic. This change may have been caused by some sadness in the writer's life (one of his twins died in 1596). Shakespeare, however, was not the only writer whose works at this time were very serious. The whole of England was facing a crisis. Queen Elizabeth I was growing old. She was greatly loved, and the people were sad to think she must soon die; they were also afraid, for the Queen had never married, and so there was no child to succeed her.

When James I came to the throne in 1603, Shakespeare continued to write serious drama—the great tragedies and the plays based on Roman history (such as *Julius Caesar*) for which he

is most famous. Finally, before he retired from the theatre, he
wrote another set of comedies. These all have the same theme:
they tell of happiness which is lost, and then found again.

Shakespeare returned from London to Stratford, his home
town. He was rich and successful, and he owned one of the biggest
houses in the town. He died in 1616.

Shakespeare also wrote two long poems, and a collection of
sonnets. The sonnets describe two love-affairs, but we do not
know who the lovers were. Although there are many public
documents concerned with his career as a writer and a business-
man, Shakespeare has hidden his personal life from us. A
nineteenth-century poet, Matthew Arnold, addressed Shakespeare
in a poem, and wrote 'We ask and ask—Thou smilest, and art
still'.

There is not even a trustworthy portrait of the world's greatest
dramatist.

Approximate order of composition of Shakespeare's works

Period	Comedies	History plays	Tragedies	Poems
I	Comedy of Errors	Henry VI, part 1	Titus Andronicus	
	Taming of the Shrew	Henry VI, part 2		
	Two Gentlemen of Verona	Henry VI, part 3		Venus and Adonis
1594		Richard III		Rape of Lucrece
	Love's Labour's Lost	King John		
II	Midsummer Night's Dream	Richard II	Romeo and Juliet	Sonnets
	Merchant of Venice	Henry IV, part 1		
	Merry Wives of Windsor	Henry IV, part 2		
1599	Much Ado About Nothing			
	As You Like It	Henry V		
III	Twelfth Night		Julius Caesar	
	Troilus and Cressida		Hamlet	
	Measure for Measure		Othello	
1608	All's Well That Ends Well		Timon of Athens	
			King Lear	
			Macbeth	
			Antony and Cleopatra	
			Coriolanus	
IV	Pericles			
	Cymbeline			
1613	The Winter's Tale	Henry VIII		
	The Tempest